The Thoughtful Researcher

Information Literacy Series

The Thoughtful Researcher: Teaching the Research Process to Middle School Students. By Virginia Rankin.

The Thoughtful Researcher

Teaching the Research Process to Middle School Students

Virginia Rankin

1999
Libraries Unlimited, Inc.
And Its Division
Teacher Ideas Press
Englewood, Colorado

For the nuns, Sisters of Charity of Halifax and
Sisters of St. Joseph, who taught me how to write,
and for David, who cheers me on and keeps me going.

The author gratefully acknowledges permission to reprint the quoted material appearing on pages 10, 15, and 25, from *Writing with Power: Techniques for Mastering the Writing Process* by Peter Elbow (New York: Oxford University Press, 1981).

Libraries Unlimited, Inc.
And Its Division
Teacher Ideas Press
P.O. Box 6633
Englewood, CO 80155-6633
1-800-237-6124
www.lu.com

Library of Congress Cataloging-in-Publication Data

Rankin, Virginia.
    The thoughtful researcher : teaching the research process to
middle school students / by Virginia Rankin.
        xvi, 211 p. 22x28 cm. -- (Information literacy series)
        Includes bibliographical references and index.
        ISBN 1-56308-698-0 (softbound)
        1. Library orientation for middle school students--United States.
I. Title. II. Series.
Z711.2.R26   1999
027.62'6--dc21   98-55916
                                                    CIP

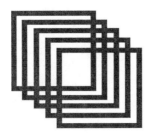

Contents

List of Handouts

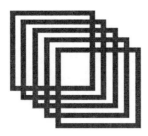

Preface

Fourteen years ago, after a move across the country, I found myself doing research on my new school district. I discovered that the teaching of thinking skills was central to the district's mission. How, I wondered, would thinking skills apply to library research? It turned out to be the most important question I have ever asked.

I began to identify a few tentative answers. Students should develop their own research questions by deciding what they wish to know. They would need time to plan research strategies, plus time to evaluate and modify their strategies. My original answers led to some new inquiries. How could students generate good questions on occasions when they would not have any prior knowledge of a topic? Once students had located information that seemed relevant to their questions, how would they make sense of it? So it has gone ever since, with a solution to an initial query inevitably leading to new subjects for investigation.

Sometimes an answer itself becomes the topic for consideration. Yes, students' own questions are crucial, but how could I ensure that their questions would be truly worth posing? In writing this book, this has sometimes meant that a particular aspect of a research process step cannot be contained within a single chapter devoted to that step. Some subjects merit a chapter all their own. Thus, question generating has emerged from a consideration of the presearch, time management from planning, reading from notetaking, and both thinking skills and the visual display of information from the creating of a quality product.

Even this sounds too tidy, for the research process is not linear; it is more like a complicated spider web. Process steps intersect and connect in many different ways. Research questions guide notetaking; notetaking can lead to new questions. Assessment should be part of every step in the research process, rather than just a summing up at the end. I have tried to make connections clear with a liberal use of cross-references throughout this book.

I do not expect ever to finish my quest to understand the research process; this book represents my best thinking at this time. I have spent more than a decade considering topics such as the presearch and notetaking. Other issues, such as search strategies, have only recently returned to my radar screen, and I find my ideas constantly evolving. I still have many unanswered questions. There are important matters on which I cannot speak at all; sadly, I have never had the opportunity to work on projects that lead to authentic products.

And what of technology? While I do not have much to say specifically about technology, almost everything in this book relates to technology. The research process should be the same no matter what kind of resources one chooses. It is more crucial than ever to teach research as a thinking process when students have access to electronic resources. Lacking an awareness of process steps, and enchanted by the technology itself, their view of research could easily shrink to the simple location and copying of information. We must not let this happen.

Whenever I have written "you" or "we," I have pictured a teacher-librarian like myself working in a middle or junior high school. But I would not have been able to write a word without the colleagues who taught in the classrooms of the four middle schools I have called home. So many of them were ready for an adventure and willing to take risks. We worked together to discover how we might teach our students to become competent researchers and independent learners. I am grateful to every one of them, and I hope that classroom teachers interested in the same quest will also find this book useful.

Special thanks go to Kathy Kellogg, the amazing art teacher mentioned several times in this book, for the maps and original drawings that grace Chapter 12.

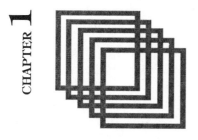

CHAPTER 1

Teaching Research in a Middle School

May You Live in Exciting Times

Middle school is undoubtedly the most overlooked area of K–12 education. Few books focus specifically on this level, and few education schools prepare teachers to teach at it. Middle school teachers must frequently adapt what the experts have to say about elementary or high school to fit their own situations. Administrators and curriculum developers tend to focus on giving students a good start in elementary school, and on preparing them for work or higher education in high school. Middle school is often seen as a period of marking time between the important tasks of the other two levels.

Nevertheless, for a teacher-librarian interested in teaching the library research process, middle school is absolutely the best place to be. The opportunities to teach the process and coach students as they apply skills and strategies are plentiful—and the students are ready to learn.

MIDDLE SCHOOL STUDENTS

Walk the hallways of any middle school, and you will see students who tower over everyone else—boys and girls who would not look out of place in a high school. Beside them you will find others so tiny it is hard to believe they are not visitors from the nearby elementary school. Nowhere is the range of physical development greater than in middle school. Yes, kindergartners are vastly different from fifth graders, and freshman from seniors, but in middle school this physical diversity can be found within each grade level, within each classroom.

Students' bodies are not just changing in size; they are changing in shape as well. It is a difficult time to live through; everyone is certain that he or she doesn't fit in. Even those who enjoy some popularity believe they can lose their status and become an outsider at any moment. Each decision—hair, clothes, sports, friends—is a big one. Make the wrong choice and the consequences could be disastrous—everyone will think you are weird.

Yet middle school is also a time of openness. I can ask my students to do just about anything, and they will. Well, okay, there are always a few grumblers, but most middle school students still see learning as an adventure. If we, as their teachers, can offer them a learning experience that looks interesting, with the potential to distract them for a moment from worrying about what everyone thinks of their hair, they are ready for it. I think their vulnerability contributes to their openness. They need to connect. If we can be there for them, asking, "How can I help?" and meaning it, they are likely to respond.

Middle school is a time of increasing intellectual capability. My students are ready for a more challenging approach to research. They do not have all the cognitive sophistication they will, with any luck, acquire in high school, but they have enough to make this a marvelous time for teaching the research process. Middle school students can pose thoughtful research questions. They can develop careful research plans, and evaluate and adjust those plans. They can locate relevant sources, and evaluate their sources. They can identify main ideas in their reading, and take summarized notes. They can construct new meaning from their research, and produce final products of real substance.

I tell my students that the research process they learn in middle school will prepare them for the assignments they will encounter in high school. This is indeed my goal. Actually, my goal is somewhat larger; I wish them to become independent, self-directed learners. To achieve this, I must do more than simply teach them the basic steps in the research process.

I want to send my students off with a well-stocked tool kit of strategies for implementing each process step. By the time they reach high school, they will have used several different note-taking formats. They will have several options when they find themselves confronted with a research assignment. They can select the notetaking approach that best suits their style, or a particular assignment. Exposing middle school students to a range of strategies for a process step also helps them develop the confidence and flexibility to use a less comfortable strategy when a teacher requires it.

Developing our students' confidence is as important as developing their skills. Instruction peppered with questions communicates the message, "You *can* do it." I enjoy designing well-organized logical instruction, but I know I must include lots of opportunities for students' input along the way. What do you already know about this? What might work here? How can we find out? What should we do next? I am always amazed at how much they already know. So, I think, are they—amazed and pleased.

This way lies the route to success; build on what students already know. For this reason, I like to use students as models whenever I can. If a class is struggling to apply a skill, having another student model the skill both clarifies and inspires.

Students must have plenty of opportunities to practice skills and strategies during actual assignments. To prepare them for upcoming tasks, we can teach students needed skills just before they begin their research. We can present mini-lessons during daily research sessions on a planned or needs-to-know basis. We can meet with students after the assignment has been completed to review successes and frustrations, and plan for next time. Every minute not spent on formal instruction should be spent coaching students as they try to apply skills.

Middle school is a high-energy, hands-on time of life for a student, so a middle school teacher-librarian must be a high energy, hands-on kind of person. If the question, "Can I help?" is used as a thinly disguised disciplinary tactic, students will recognize it for what it is and reject it. Tell your students that you will be their coach, and that you will work with them throughout their research to help them master the process. Demonstrate that you mean this not only by offering assistance, but also by asking probing questions to make sure students are on track. Students will see you as a person who helps, and you will have plenty of requests for your services.

Of course, you will need the cooperation of classroom teachers to make this a reality. Once again, we who work at the middle school level have a wonderful opportunity.

MIDDLE SCHOOL TEACHERS

In far too many elementary schools, library time for students equals planning time for teachers. They deliver their students to the teacher-librarian for a weekly dose of library science or literature, then scurry off to the coffee pot or photocopy machine. Those who are willing to collaborate on a research project may find the way blocked by an inflexible library schedule. I admire my elementary school colleagues who struggle so valiantly to come up with solutions.

High school librarians, on the other hand, are likely to have flexible schedules and therefore libraries full of students. Collaborative partners who will work with them in teaching the research process are harder to find. Some are willing to have the librarian teach an occasional class, but that is as far as many are willing to go. Focused on covering their curriculum, teachers may feel they can "spare" only a day or two of class time for library work. Others expect students to complete research projects entirely on their own time. Such an approach keeps the teacher-librarian busy working with individual students, but it is not an efficient use of his or her time, and many students may receive no assistance of any sort.

There are certainly many elementary and high school libraries with exemplary programs, but the problems I have outlined are common at both levels. By contrast, middle schools frequently offer an almost perfect set of circumstances for teaching the research process.

It has been my experience that most middle school teachers regard library research as an integral part of their programs. Given the hands-on nature of their students, they are looking for assignments that allow students to work independently or in small groups, and to have some control over their own learning. A resource-based project in the library meets these criteria.

The word *project* is important. Middle school teachers are usually not wedded to the idea that research must inevitably lead to a formal, lengthy paper. A good thing too, for one such paper a year is usually enough to exhaust both teacher and students. Because teachers are willing to try a variety of approaches to research and a variety of types and sizes of final products, they are more likely to use the library on a regular and frequent basis.

Thus, middle school teacher-librarians are presented with many openings for teaching and coaching different aspects of the research process. We do not need to cram everything into a few days of instruction per year—an approach that is doomed from the start. We can choose to emphasize one step in the research process with one assignment, and a different step with another. We can build on and reinforce strategies we have already taught. We can make connections between different stages of the research process. We can teach for transfer from one discipline to another, showing students that strategies learned during a social studies project will also help during science research.

It has also been my experience that middle school teachers are likely to see themselves as instructional partners in a research project. Of course, there will always be a few who will see library time as a chance to correct papers or make phone calls. However, most teachers, with only a little tactful prompting, will circulate among their students, offering help when it is needed. When they confer with us about a specific student's problems, we can offer useful models for coaching the research process. When they see us working just as hard as they are, they will realize that together we can accomplish twice as much.

COLLABORATIVE PLANNING

Of course, I want much more than just assistance while students are engaged in doing research; I want to be included in the planning of research assignments from the very beginning. In the best of all possible worlds, every teacher would approach me well before the start of an assignment. Together we would identify instructional goals and assessment criteria to reinforce those goals. We would discern prerequisite skills and knowledge and divide instructional responsibilities. At the completion of the assignment, we would review what went well and what went poorly, and make plans for what we might do differently next time.

In my less-than-ideal world, I have often considered myself lucky to receive any prior notice at all of an upcoming assignment. For a while, I found consolation in the few partners who did ask for my help when their research projects were nothing more than vague ideas just beginning to gel. One day I realized I would make more progress if I relaxed a bit about my ideal for collaboration. I did not expect my students to master a new skill instantly or to progress at the same speeds. Why should I expect this of teachers?

I began to see teachers as ranged along a continuum of collaboration, and I began to believe I could move them along that continuum. Some, with just a little encouragement, progressed rapidly. For others, every small step was a triumph. It is best to take the long view in working with those who start at zero on the continuum. I must remind myself how much progress they have made over several years; yes, they are only at three, but they used to be at zero. I am excited when a teacher, who has never before given me a copy of an assignment, suddenly thinks of slipping one in my mailbox.

After I realized that every collaboration did not have to match the ideal, I was free to consider how I might become more involved in planning with a variety of teachers.

One of my first breakthroughs came with a veteran teacher. I could set my watch by her. It's December; it must be time to do "historical celebrity press conferences." She had developed this assignment fifteen years before, and she was still very proud of it. She loved getting out all the props—press corps badges and old microphones. And this project certainly had its good points; it was far superior to the standard dry biographical report.

So I would grit my teeth when I saw her students coming, and prepare for an hour of explaining to student after student what a "significant achievement" might be. Their teacher, passing by, would growl, "I told you all about that back in the classroom." When not explaining significant achievements, I would probably be attempting to redirect students who were absorbed in figuring out the number of children their historical celebrities had, or their husbands' or wives' names—unlikely topics for a press conference.

I expected to be doing the same thing every December. Then one winter, this teacher confessed that her students had not done as well as in past years, and actually neither had last year's group. In my school, we have seen a noticeable decline in students' skills. Many veteran teachers have been frustrated in their attempts to provide students with successful learning experiences. This very real problem has led to some opportunities for me.

In this case, I suggested that many of her students might never have seen a press conference. Perhaps we ought to tape the president's next one to show the following year; then students would have a model of what they were aiming for. I agreed that the assignment questions were great, but suggested students' understanding might increase if they generated the questions themselves. I confidently promised her that their questions would be quite similar to those on her list. I offered to help one section develop their questions so that she would know how to do it with the rest of her classes. The following year, when we tried this, things went so well that I suggested we also work together to coach students in oral presentation skills.

It takes tact to critique a research assignment with a teacher, especially when you were not involved in the initial planning. This veteran teacher gave me an opening when she voiced her doubts; she appeared to be inviting discussion of her project. Often, after a disappointing project, the last thing a teacher wants to hear is anything that sounds like criticism. However, when I have spent a considerable amount of time helping students with a project, I yearn to give the teacher suggestions that will make the experience more successful for the next class.

September is a good time to offer teachers suggestions about an assignment that they will probably be giving again in the coming year. In September, we all have the highest hopes. Teachers are more likely to feel flattered that I have been thinking about them rather than threatened because they feel I might be criticizing their work.

Unfortunately, in some cases, no approach is gentle enough. Some teachers will resist even the smallest gesture toward collaboration. One teacher, angry with my request for a copy of her assignment, told me that she would never work with me, and advised me to simply leave her alone. It turned out to be the best advice she could have given me. I am usually not a quitter, but I decided to give up on this teacher. Of course, I continued to do my best to assist her students whenever they were in the library. Three years later, she strode into my office and announced that she wanted to try something new; she wondered if I would like to help.

I learned something from this experience. For a few teachers, my desire for a collaborative relationship will feel like pressure. And they will resist it. If I abandon the hope that our relationship can grow and simply meet this teacher on his or her own terms, sooner or later—probably later—something good may happen.

Teachers fresh out of college present a special problem. In their training, they have probably learned nothing about teaching students to do research. Their only models are memories of assignments they themselves received in middle school or junior high.

One such teacher, giving his first research assignment, concentrated on externals: a cover, a table of contents, a bibliography. The assignment was to research "anything that has a history." His only attempt to focus the research was the concept of chronological chapters commencing in prehistory. Students interested in modern technology, things like cars and computers, presented one problem. Those with broad topics, like sports and art, another. The ensuing chaos told him he was in trouble, but he also felt very defensive.

This was a semester-long project, with students spending one week in the library each month. This could not be ignored, nor could it wait until September. He needed help, or it was going to be a very long semester for everyone. He looked unhappy when I suggested we talk, and he approached our conference with all the enthusiasm of one about to be sent before a firing squad. Do not be put off by the defensiveness of a beginner; it has not yet hardened into the shell that surrounds some veterans. He relaxed as soon as he realized I wanted to help.

I had collected a variety of well-designed assignments and assessment criteria. Because he had some choices, he did not feel I was pressuring him to do research my way, the one right way. His choices were not the ones I would have made, but every model I had given him was an acceptable one.

After this experience, I realized that most teachers could use good examples of assessment criteria for research projects. I assembled as many as I could into a booklet that I distributed to the entire faculty. I keep a copy handy in my office for those teachable moments when someone sits down to plan an assignment with me.

The assessment booklet led to the concept of a menu of choices for each step in the research process. If I want to encourage a teacher to use a presearch, I present a variety of techniques, then let him decide the one that fits his assignment best. If a teacher mentions notetaking, we can consider a variety of formats that her students might use. If another confides that her students' notes are excellent, but their final products humdrum, we can review some thinking skills options that will lead to a more creative use of information. You can use this book as a collection of menus for each step in the research process. Share them with collaborative partners, and expand them by adding your own ideas.

RESEARCH AS A PROCESS

If your teachers are unfamiliar with the concept of the research process, you may want to begin by sharing examples of the process approach. Several years ago, my school decided, as part of a broader process of school reform, to define expectations for library research. A committee reviewed more than a dozen different models of the research process. These came from a variety of states and Canadian provinces as well as from individual authors. Some had five steps, some six, some as many as nine or ten. We finally settled upon eight steps ourselves, but we did not insist that our version was perfect, merely that it made the most sense to us.

The results of that work form the basis of the "Research Steps and Strategies Checklist" to be found in Chapter 5. I have not placed the checklist at the front of this book, because I am not trying to sell it. I believe it is important for everyone to understand that research is a process, and to subscribe to some model of that process. The different versions of the research process have more commonalties than differences; the differences tend to be ones of emphasis. Different processes pay greater attention to certain steps, and articulate more precisely the tasks to be performed during those steps. At my school, we felt lucky to be able to examine so many different models and to select from among the particular strengths of each.

Realistically, not many schools will have the chance to put together their own delineation of the research process. While ownership may not be as strong initially, the next best thing is to have a particular process adopted by your district or state. If you have an "official" process, don't let the teacher-librarian be the only one who knows about it. If neither your school, district, nor state has adopted a process, find a model you feel comfortable with and share it with your teachers. In-services are good; posters outlining the process are good; but you must also refer to this process whenever you plan with a teacher.

I do not mean that you need to review the entire process before every assignment. I rarely emphasize more than one or two process steps for any research project. Unless an assignment has a lengthy time line, that will be all students can master. Often the assignment itself will call for skill development at a specific step. Search strategies will facilitate the location of hard-to-find resources. Critical thinking skills will help students evaluate information on controversial topics. A presearch will give researchers background knowledge about unfamiliar subjects. Sometimes a class's past performance will indicate that students need further coaching, as well as some new strategies, in an area like question generating or notetaking.

Whenever you present teachers with a menu of choices for one pro-cess step, do present that step as part of a complete research process. Point out that a particular step seems important right now, and give the reason you will not be placing as much emphasis on others. As the school year progresses and new assignments come along, indicate how you can still build on and reinforce strategies for previously introduced steps, even though you will shift the main focus to a new step.

A RENEWED VISION

Our goal is a school where all teachers share a vision of what it means to be a thoughtful researcher. Achieving the vision calls for each teacher to share in the task of developing competent researchers. Sometimes, we may taste success when a grade level, or a department, or even a whole school determines exactly who will be responsible for teaching what.

Our success may endure for a year or two or three, but in the end, change is the only constant. We may hear that the incoming sixth graders, despite the best efforts of their elementary teachers, do not possess some of the competencies we have come to expect. Some key instructional lead-ers may retire or move to Australia. Those of us left behind are different, too. We know things now, about learning and teaching, that we did not know three years ago.

We need to keep renewing our vision, and revising the road map we have designed to get us there. We must remember to pull out the document that looked so good two or three years ago. What still looks good? Where are the holes? What do we want to discard? We must be reflective practitio-ners. We must decide anew what we want our students to know and what learning experiences will lead them to become thoughtful researchers.

CHAPTER 2

Becoming a
Reflective Practitioner

Change Is the Only Constant

I recently stumbled upon an old folder of notes taken during a workshop with Carol Kuhlthau. The first thing I had written was, "No such thing as a perfect librarian." I think those words were important to me because I had once believed in an ideal that I could find—probably in a book or perhaps at a conference—and then become. Kuhlthau wanted to share a much more exciting possibility. My notes continue, "Be a reflective practitioner. Develop an environment that enables you to grow."

This book contains ideas developed from my reflections on the research process. As I progress through another school year, I know that I will continue to reflect, and that some of these ideas will change; some will expand or metamorphose; some I may discard. I hope that you will also take these ideas and modify them, use them as jumping off points to help you break through to something new.

The knowledge that I will never reach some satisfying end point, where I know everything I need to know, is scary, but it is also comforting. Change is the only constant in teaching and in the library. As surely as the computer on my desk will change, my students will change. The curriculum will change. The colleagues I work with will change and never be quite the same group from year to year. It is reassuring to know that I have some techniques and habits of mind that will help me deal with the changes life is sure to send my way. It is also liberating to believe that I don't need to know "everything" to teach a skill or strategy. Through my teaching, I will learn more of what I need to know and do. It is a neverending process.

SUBJECTS FOR REFLECTION

When we reflect upon something, the dictionary tells us that we consider that thing seriously. We ponder, contemplate, study, meditate, muse, speculate. The central question for me, as a teacher-librarian, is how can I best help my students become thoughtful researchers? The perspective from which I consider this question will influence the kinds of answers I find. I can consider my own teaching, both in style and substance. I can study how different types of students learn best. I can look at a specific class, and ponder how I might tailor instruction to meet their skills and needs.

Elbow (1981, 131) notes that

> The mark of the person who can actually make *progress* in thinking . . . is a willingness to notice and listen to these inconvenient little details, these annoying loose ends, these embarrassments or puzzles, instead of impatiently sweeping them under the rug. A good new idea looks obvious and inevitable *after* it is all worked out and the dust has settled, but in the beginning it just feels annoying and the wrong old idea feels persuasively correct.

The subjects I choose for reflection often come from those "inconvenient little details," "annoying loose ends," and "embarrassments or puzzles."

Elbow (1981, 134) also refers to "messes," and declares, "If these messes never happen to you, perhaps you are not listening sympathetically enough to pesky examples and contrary arguments." The ability to listen sympathetically and acknowledge the messes comes from a kind of insecurity—my teaching isn't good enough; I've got to make it better. It also comes from a deeper sense of security—if I try to improve, I will be successful; it's worth the effort.

Reflecting on Teaching

My earliest reflections focused on the substance of what I taught, the content. My successes in teaching research as a thinking process were punctuated by "aha" moments. One day I realized that my students could locate useful resources, but once the thrill of searching was over, they could not think of anything to do but copy from them. Aha, I needed to learn everything I could about notetaking. But later, when they could summarize and find main ideas, they still were not sure which main ideas to record. Aha, I needed to . . . Well, at first, I was not exactly sure what I needed to do.

A reflection can begin that way, with just a nagging worry that something is missing. After some contemplating, meditating, and musing, I realized that something *before* notetaking was missing. I began to envision how students might engage in a presearch that would lead them to ask focused questions, and thus to a sense of *what* main ideas to record. So far so good, but some students needed more help with posing good questions, and the presearches I had developed did not work in every research situation. There will always be issues related to the teaching of the research process to ponder and study.

Sometimes the substance of what I am trying to teach is right on target, and yet I still miss the mark. I began to consider my style of teaching the day a student dramatically declared, "This is *so* boring." But wait, I had taught this skill this way before—that very morning in fact—and I had never before had problems. Looking out at this class, though, I could see this one daring girl was telling the truth as they all saw it; they *were* bored. Their apologetic teacher tried to console me later by explaining that they always had trouble sitting still. Well, I thought, surely there are ways to teach these students without requiring them to sit still for extended periods. I began to think about the needs of kinesthetic learners. Now I am constantly looking for kinesthetic activities, such as the "Kinesthetic KWL" (see Chapter 3) and "Notes on Gummed Sheets" (see Chapter 9). This is not my own learning style, so it is hard work for me.

Classes that do not like to sit still usually do like to talk, but a lecture-dialogue format does not give everybody enough opportunity to express his or her ideas. This realization sent me on another seemingly never-ending quest, this time for cooperative learning activities that work well with my instructional goals. Luckily, quite a bit more attention has been given to cooperative activities than to kinesthetic learning, so this is an easier task.

Reflecting on Students

There is simply no time to lament that the students I have today are not like the students of years past. If I am to teach all students well, I must have a sense of who *these* students are. Sometimes they are quite willing to tell me about themselves if I can just remember to ask. I usually ask as many questions as I answer during sixth-grade orientation. "What do you want to know about this library?" led to a discovery I have now confirmed many times over. Incoming sixth graders are mourning the loss of a smaller elementary library they have come to know intimately, and a librarian who provided lots of individual "service." Knowing this, I have made reassuring my new students a major focus of orientation. Yes, this library is bigger, and often quite busy, so you may have to ask for help when you need it, but the fun part of my job is helping *you*. I also announce that I have a three-year plan to teach all the research skills they will need to move on to the even bigger high school library.

The self-assessment forms that students complete at the end of a research unit can also give me a clearer understanding of their needs. I often include a question asking how the teaching of research skills could be improved. Many students just scrawl, "I don't know." But I will occasionally get a good lead, such as, "I needed more help with how I used my time." I know I have something to ponder when better use of time also keeps turning up in response to the query, "What would you do differently if you were starting over?"

Classroom teachers sometimes provide a student-centered topic for reflection. The lead teacher in our "extremely gifted program" (IQs above 142) asked me to consider what his students needed to know to become better researchers. He had begun by accepting their own estimate that they already knew everything about research but had become increasingly frustrated by the slapdash quality of their work. He gave me two months to come up with some answers; then we would collaborate on a research unit. Until then, students would continue to do research independently with no instruction from me.

Informal observations of how these gifted students carried out research in the library led me to some conclusions about what they needed to know and how I might go about teaching them. I quickly deduced that, for most, a successful search meant accumulating the largest number of resources; few stopped to consider relevancy, currency, or depth of coverage. I also realized that I would have to insert mini-lessons into their actual research. Their own opinions of their abilities would not allow them to sit still for anything that looked like formal library instruction. I could begin a mini-lesson with an introduction such as, "I see many of you are having difficulties locating detailed, up-to-date information. I have some tips that can help." Or better yet, "Charles (already coached through a process by me) is going to show you some things that have worked for him."

From time to time, I like to take a more in-depth look at individual students. In the case of gifted students, I could follow several selected ones through a series of research projects to learn more about their needs and how I might help them. Sometimes I identify students for a closer look not by some label they have received, but by the results I see—they never complete their research, or their research is always of poor quality.

Reflecting on Individual Classes

Coaches in team sports like to talk about having a game plan. The game plan varies depending on the strengths and weaknesses of the opponent; having a game plan works better than playing every opposing team exactly the same way. Because I have found the game plan a useful concept for teaching, I like to do a little basic research on any class before I work with them for the first time.

I start by asking their teacher some questions. How big is the class? In my district, where class size can be quite large, I have learned that techniques that work well with a class of 22 often do not work with a class of 35. Because classes are not always balanced by gender, I inquire about the number of males and females. For a class of 25 boys, I warm up beforehand, so that I am ready to speak loudly and to move more than usual. I also remember not to leave out the four subdued girls. Sometimes it helps me to see a class roster. I may never have worked with this social studies class, but if I have seen most of the students together in their science section, I have an idea of their abilities and style.

Teachers, asked to describe their classes, will often declare one "good" and another "bad." I try to get at the nature of this so-called goodness and badness by looking for specifics. Is the teacher referring to skills or behavior? The two do not necessarily go together. There is often intellectual gold to be mined in rowdy classes. When describing a class afraid to take any risks for fear of failing, teachers sometimes use *well-behaved* as a synonym for *passive*. I find it useful to ask for concrete examples of a class's notable successes or outright disasters. I also want to know if the teacher can suggest particular strategies that seem to work well with a specific class.

If a coach is lucky, the game plan works; if it does not work, the coach has to make adjustments—while playing. This is also the lot of a teacher-librarian. Sometimes, despite my best efforts to prepare for a class, I realize as I work with the students that I am not "winning." In some cases, I can identify the problem by comparing them to another class in which the same approach is working quite well. The comparison may reveal that the successful class possesses a prerequisite skill that the struggling class does not; perhaps there are several missing skills. If the classes have different teachers, the differences can sometimes be traced to classroom preparation. Perhaps one teacher spent more time on needed skills, or focused on motivating the class before the research assignment. One group may be used to working cooperatively (or independently) and the other may not. Sometimes I find that I am asking for a degree of rigor that a class is not used to.

No matter what conclusions I draw, I must next face the question, what do I do now? When I have more time to reflect, I can also ask, what will I do the next time I work with these students, or the next time I work with this teacher?

TECHNIQUES FOR REFLECTION

As a reflective practitioner, I am always gathering data. If my students are confused or floundering or resistant, I look for clues to help me understand why. If things are going well, I try to identify the key factors in this success, so that I do not have to reinvent the wheel next time. Over the years, I have managed to identify a number of techniques that help me ponder my questions about how I can help students learn.

Task Analysis

Some years ago, when I concluded that I needed to do a better job when teaching my students to take notes, I also realized that I did not know exactly what it was that I had to teach them. My own notetaking served me reasonably well, but I had never stopped to reflect on exactly how I did it. I had recently learned how to do a task analysis (see Fig. 2.1, p. 14) in a class on thinking skills with Barry Beyer. We had used this technique to identify the steps involved in the execution of a particular skill (Beyer 1987). Now I decided I would take notes and watch how I did it. I also asked some friends whose jobs involved research to do the same thing. One returned a page of notes taken in blue ink with comments on her process in red. A six-step notetaking process began to emerge (see Fig. 9.4, p. 106), but something still seemed to be missing. After about a year of helping students work with the process, I knew what it was, and added the seventh step.

I had been struggling for some time with the question of how to teach students to read information when I found myself spontaneously engaging in a task analysis. I was reading a magazine article, and the material was challenging. I began watching myself closely to see precisely what I did as I read. I jotted down every strategy I used to understand the information in that article, and ended up with ten. Encouraged by my success, I moved on to an even more confusing article on economics. I realized that my own reading strategies were automatic and unconscious; to bring them out in the open where I could become aware of them, I needed to work with challenging material.

When I have an "aha" moment and realize that my students are missing a needed research skill, my first step is often to try a task analysis. One application of a skill is never enough to determine all that is involved. I need to do several task analyses to ferret out steps I may have initially missed. A skill can also look slightly different depending on my purpose and the complexity of the material I am working with.

Fig. 2.1. Task Analysis of Research Skills

1. Attempt to execute the skill.

2. Watch what you or a partner do, using:
   • in-process observation
   • memory
   • audio or videotape

3. If the skill is easy for you, use a challenging situation.

4. After the initial analysis, be on the lookout for missing steps.

5. Remember, knowledge of an operation will change, depending on:
   • purpose
   • complexity of data
   • level of experience

Focus Folders

There are times when I am not quite sure exactly what I am looking for; I just know that something is missing. I may have only a broad general question, such as, what can I do to help my students improve the quality of their final products? This kind of question will emerge in different ways with different classes. It identifies a problem that cannot be resolved with a single strategy. When such a question becomes important to me, I find myself having ideas about it all the time. In my early years as a teacher-librarian, those ideas disappeared just as quickly as they appeared. If I waited until the end of the day to jot down an idea, I found I could no longer remember what had seemed like an unforgettable inspiration only a few hours before.

I finally realized that I needed to write down my ideas as soon as possible. I now scribble brainstorms on the corners of handouts while in the midst of a busy class. I can be seen snatching scrap paper from recycle bins to jot down a few words that will jog my memory later. If a thought comes to me at lunch, it may end up on a scrap of brown bag or a napkin. I record everything—nagging questions as well as brilliant perceptions. At the end of the day, I clean out my pockets and see what I've written. On some days, I may find two or three notes; on others, nothing at all. I look to see if my writing is too cryptic to be understood later on, and add clarifying words if needed.

The next step is to drop my notes into a folder labeled "quality products," or "time management," or whatever the question of the moment may be. Then I forget about what I have written—usually for months. When I finally open the folder and sort through all my notes I am amazed at how much I now know. All I needed to do was keep the question in mind and be alert for anything that might extend my understanding. Almost always, my thoughts can be organized into three or four main categories; I have gone from confusion and disorientation to a rough map of the landscape for the topic under study. I find that some ideas come up repeatedly in slightly different forms; these are usually important signposts to a solution.

For me, the next step will be writing, but not the sort of writing you are reading right now. I write to see what I really think and to push further the beginnings of ideas.

Directed Freewriting

I am not sure who first came up with the idea of freewriting, but I am extremely grateful to him or her. It is simply the best way I know of to think. Even if you do not like to write, you will find freewriting useful if you approach it as a thinking tool.

Natalie Goldberg (1990, 1–5) has done an excellent job of clarifying "the rules" of this approach. You must keep your hand moving; this allows you to escape your inner critic. You will be helped in this great escape by the knowledge that you are not to worry about spelling, punctuation, or grammar. Having given your inner critic the slip, the next step is to lose control. Goldberg (1990, 3) advises not worrying about the correctness or appropriateness of your thoughts. I have learned that it is okay, even productive, to write down my hesitancies, confusion, and fears. Elbow (1981, 13) also gives you permission to move from one topic to another.

Goldberg (1986) insists that you must not think, by which she means you are not to settle for the first ideas that come to mind. Why not? Elbow (1981, 43) issues this warning:

> Even when you do manage to decide on your meaning before you start writing, and you feel satisfied with it . . . , sticking with that meaning as you write stops all creativity and the generation of new ideas. You have settled for what you already know and understand. You have locked yourself into duller thinking than you are really capable of; indeed, you have virtually ruled out your best thinking.

I always have a starting point when I begin a freewrite; this is a topic I am interested in exploring. I may also start with a framework for considering that topic, such as my prejudices, or a dialogue that expresses conflicting points of view. Elbow (1981, 61–73) provides a treasure trove of these frameworks.

Freewriting is usually timed, but you can make the time any length you wish. Mine range from ten minutes to an hour. My best thinking often comes at the end of a freewrite, when I may have wandered quite far afield from my starting point. This has happened so often that I now begin freewriting with a sense of expectancy. Where will I end up this time? Not every freewrite leads to pure gold, but most contain something useful, perhaps just a single sentence that I will want to make the starting point for my next freewrite.

Freewrites often prime my mental pump. I suddenly start having all sorts of new ideas when I am far from my notebook—and that is where index cards come in handy.

Inspiration Card Files

This is such a good, simple idea that I wish I could take credit for it, but if I had not read *Bird by Bird* by Anne Lamott (1994), I would still be letting some of my best ideas fly away. She suggests having a supply of index cards everywhere that inspiration might strike, for instance, the kitchen, the bathroom, next to your bed, in the car, etc.

Sitting down to tackle a problem or develop a new approach can be scary. The beauty of the cards is that they allow ideas to sneak up on me. And practice makes perfect with this approach. If I allow my mind to stay open to brainstorms, I find I have more and more of them. I can even set my brain to receive them. I expect to have new ideas whenever I set out on a solitary walk. Every jacket I own has its supply of cards.

I have added my own wrinkles to Lamott's basic idea. I use brightly colored cards because they are harder to misplace. She does not impose any organization on her cards; I find it very reassuring to sort mine by topic in a little card file. I do agree with what I believe is her reason for treating her cards in such a casual way. The cards are "inspiration as no big deal." I am not waiting for something worthy of engraving on stone tablets. If I have a brainstorm, I write it down. If I later decide it's worthless, I toss it out; it's only a card.

Case Studies

Index cards are a relaxed approach to inquiry. Case studies, by contrast, require a serious commitment. The strategies I use are inspired by the work of Eleanor Duckworth (1987), who wants teachers to be like Piaget, observing a few individual students closely to see how they go about solving problems. When I do a case study, I look at how students solve problems connected with doing research. I try to ask questions that do not reveal hoped for answers, and to listen more than I talk. I am not interested in whether a student's approach is right or wrong; I want to understand how students think and how they try to make sense of a problem.

I find a case study worthwhile when I have a compelling question about how students do research. My very first case study was triggered by a perception that successful students felt comfortable asking for help during the research process, while students who did poorly usually did not ask for help. I could see many possible explanations. Low-achieving students did not want to be seen as inadequate. They did not expect to get help if they asked for it. They thought it was cheating to ask for help. They considered research a worthless activity and so did not care. They were influenced by something in their class climate because low achievers were often grouped together. A case study seemed my best hope of finding some answers (Rankin 1992).

Once I have a focusing question, I need to decide how I will collect my data. Interviews are almost always useful. I like to speak with students before, during, and after their research. My questions will vary, but I usually try to discover their attitudes toward research by asking them to describe previous research projects. A number of questions help me understand their processes. "Tell me what you did when . . . " "Can you tell me what you were thinking when . . .?" "Why do you think that happened?" "Did you consider any other possibilities?" "Would you do anything differently now?" "Tell me more about that." "What do you like best about doing research?" "What do you like least?"

In addition to interviews, I will select at least one other method of gathering information. Journals (see Chapter 5) offer a good view of what students are thinking during the research process. If everyone in the class is keeping a journal, I can compare other students' responses to those of the case study students. Search logs also provide in-process data. I often find myself acutely aware of the students I am studying and sometimes am able to make observations as they carry out their research in the library. Time lines and flow charts of the sort designed by Carol Kuhlthau (1994) can also prove useful.

I try to choose a cooperating teacher who will be interested in my study. After all, I depend on this person to release students for interviews, and he or she is also likely to select the students I study. In my very first case study, I asked only for low achievers and high achievers, and realized too late that the high achievers were girls and the low achievers were boys. Now I am careful to warn against selecting all the students from a single gender or race or ethnic group. It is also important to define the qualities I am looking for in these students. For example, for a study of extremely gifted students, I might want to compare differences in approach between students whose gifts are primarily verbal and those whose gifts are primarily mathematical.

Interesting question, huh? That's the appeal of this approach; I can explore complex and intriguing questions about students as learners. But although the question may be of Ph.D. caliber, the investigation I carry out will not be. I am not doing scholarly research, but my close-up view of student learning offers many rewards. After my very first interviews, I was astonished by the things my students had told me. I kept exclaiming, "I can't believe I never thought to ask a student what he saw going on when he did research." When I compare the data I have gathered with my original hypotheses, I usually find that some have been supported and others ruled out. For others, I may simply have insufficient evidence.

Once I have a clearer view of the issues involved, I am ready to look for solutions. Over time, some will prove workable and become part of my instructional approach; others will be discarded. Looking back at a case study done several years ago, I was pleased to see that some of the strategies I had identified were now automatic; I had even forgotten their source. While case studies require a serious commitment of time, thought, and energy, I find them a powerful tool to help me meet the learning needs of my students. Figure 2.2 presents a summary of the steps involved in a case study.

Fig. 2.2. Planning a Case Study

1. Find a focusing question and possible hypotheses

2. Choose techniques for collection of data

3. Find a cooperating teacher

4. Select students to be observed

5. Collect data

6. Examine data for evidence and compare with hypotheses

7. Draw conclusions

8. Design solutions

Reading

I often use other reflective techniques in combination with my professional reading. After reading an article, or even better, several articles on a topic that concerns me, I like to do some freewriting. I may just mull over my responses in a general way, or I may stage a debate between different authors and let them thrash out their differences. On another day, it may be more productive for me to set off on a walk with my pocket full of index cards. As I stroll, I will wait for inspirations that help me build on an author's ideas and apply them to my situation. On other occasions, I may want a more focused approach, so I'll try a task analysis to see if I agree with an author's breakdown of a particular skill.

My own thought processes are often stimulated when I can read several different views on the same topic. If the topic is currently receiving lots of attention, I will open a folder and file everything on the subject until I have several articles—and until I have time to consider the information carefully. If I need some information right away, or I am interested in a subject that is not receiving much attention in the publications I subscribe to, I will do an ERIC search. ERIC searches often expose me to ideas from different vantage points; I can find out what science teachers and history professors think about generating good questions.

Indeed, the ideas that most enrich my teaching often come from very far afield. Writing manuals have given me useful methods for everything from topic selection to revision. Many of my best strategies for coaching my students come straight from the sports pages of the newspaper. I assume that useful information on both teaching and research can be found almost anywhere; I just need to be alert enough to recognize it when it turns up.

Debriefing with Collaborative Partners

My collaborative partners are one of my most reliable sources of good information. It is often difficult to persuade teachers to take the time to collaboratively plan a research unit; it can be nearly impossible to get them to review a unit once it has been completed. This final step is absolutely necessary, so I have devised some techniques for debriefing on-the-fly. Teachers are often acutely aware of what needs to be improved as they grade projects. I try to catch teachers while they are grading and scribble a few notes on what they tell me. This is easy to do when the projects are displays that must be graded at school. If the final products are oral presentations, I try to sit in on some of them. If they are written, I read some, and use my observations to start a conversation.

Not all assessment of a unit must be done at the end. If students are in the midst of notetaking, and my partner suddenly declares that he wishes he had reviewed categorizing, I write this down. I record every thought we have about how instruction could be improved. I file these thoughts and pull them out to consider either when we do this particular unit again, or when I work with these students again. If I plan to do the former, I put my notes in a folder labeled with the name of the unit; if the latter, they go into a folder with the teacher's name and the class period. I am steadfastly optimistic that I can improve my next teaching experience by learning from the last one.

USEFUL HABITS OF MIND

Hopefulness

I am a born optimist; I routinely see half-full glasses of water, so I feel uncomfortable preaching to anyone who is likely to perceive them as half empty. However, I do believe hopefulness is the most basic attitude of a reflective practitioner. I expect the energy I put into reflection to yield a positive outcome. Hopefulness keeps me going when my initial inquiries yield no answers and when promising answers turn out to be dead ends.

Persistence

Sometimes, when I am trying to find the solution to a big question, it feels as if I am wrestling with a bear. Then I stop and tell myself how good I am going to feel when I am finally sitting on top of that bear. Sometimes it takes years to get there, but there is nothing so exhilarating as finally overcoming an obstacle to learning. Each year I learn a bit more and advance a bit further toward my goal, whether it is teaching notetaking or meeting the needs of kinesthetic learners. Occasionally I put an issue on the back burner for a while, and that may be the best place for it at that moment, but I almost never admit defeat.

Inquisitiveness

I may fail initially, despite a hopeful attitude and dogged determination, because I am not asking the right question, or because I am missing some essential sub-questions. Inquisitiveness keeps me asking questions, looking for elements I may have missed. Finding the right question can be as exciting as finding the right answer.

Flexibility

Finding the right question often requires the flexibility to look at things in a slightly different way. I also need to be flexible enough to try different approaches, and abandon a strategy that once worked well but doesn't anymore. Or to see that because a certain strategy may not work in all situations, I will have to make adjustments when working with this teacher, or these students, or this kind of assignment.

Risk Taking

Fear can hold me back. What if I make adjustments, and they do not work? What if I spend time on an inquiry, and it does not produce anything useful? I tell my students that they should not be afraid to try something just because they might fail; they can learn from their failures. I need to believe this, too. Costa (1996) explains why risk taking is so productive. "Because (risk-takers) are constantly experimenting and experiencing, they fail frequently—but they *fail forward*, learning from the situation." The words "constantly" and "frequently" are important. The more risks we take, the easier it becomes.

THE REWARDS

Reflective practice begins with openness. I must be able to recognize that something is not working as well as it might. Perhaps an essential skill is missing, or the strategies for employing it are not fully worked out. Possibly a different instructional approach may be required to meet the needs of a particular group of learners. Maybe I just have a persistent feeling that for this unit or this class of students something is missing. Sometimes the questions I identify are complex, my study of them lengthy, and the solutions I choose extensive. However, in many cases, a relatively brief exploration and some minor changes bring major results. As a professional who is a life-long learner and problem solver, I am able to model for my students the very behaviors and attitudes I want them to develop. And I enjoy the confidence that comes from feeling that I can continually improve my teaching.

REFERENCES

Beyer, Barry K. 1987. *Practical strategies for the teaching of thinking.* Boston: Allyn & Bacon. 52, 54–57.

Costa, Arthur L. 1996. Prologue in *Visual tools for constructing knowledge* by David Hyerle. Alexandria, VA: Association for Supervision and Curriculum Development. xiii.

Duckworth, Eleanor. 1987. *"The having of wonderful ideas" & other essays on teaching & learning.* New York: Teachers College Press. 83–97.

Elbow, Peter. 1981. *Writing with power: Techniques for mastering the writing process.* New York: Oxford University Press.

Goldberg, Natalie. 1990. *Wild mind: Living the writer's life.* New York: Bantam.

——. 1986. *Writing down the bones: Freeing the writer within.* Boston: Shambhala. 8–10.

Kuhlthau, Carol Collier. 1994. *Teaching the library research process.* 2d ed. Metuchen, NJ: Scarecrow Press. 176–77, 179–86.

Lamott, Anne. 1994. *Bird by bird: Some instructions on writing and life.* New York: Anchor Books/Doubleday. 133–44.

Rankin, Virginia. 1992. A wonderful idea for the library resource center: Piagetian theories applied to library research. *Emergency Librarian* 20 (November–December): 28–32.

CHAPTER 3

Performing a Presearch

Build on a Solid Foundation

What was "Jim Crow"? Olivia *needed* to know. She had begun by wondering how prejudice and discrimination had affected Marian Anderson. The book Olivia was reading offered only a brief explanation of Jim Crow. She would have to find other sources, ones that told the story of discrimination in America. A few days later, answering a friend's inquiries about her research, she declared, "I don't think you can really understand what Anderson went through unless I explain Jim Crow."

Olivia chose Marian Anderson as her topic knowing only that she was African American and an opera singer; both things attracted her. With her classmates, she spent one class period reading brief "overviews" about her topic to expand her knowledge, and another period figuring out in detail what she wanted to know. When she began to pursue her research questions, Olivia really wanted to know more, even if it meant extending her initial search to find new resources, and even if it meant laboring over some challenging prose. If students do not have the opportunity to develop their own research questions, as Olivia did, they are likely to remain unengaged, simply going through the motions of researching without caring what they may find.

PRESEARCH STRATEGIES

Before I understood this, I used to welcome students at the start of a library assignment with a grand show-and-tell of all the resources that might help them. There would be some glazed eyes during my presentation, but once the class was turned loose, almost everyone would earnestly pursue those resources. For the first few days the library would be a pleasurable blur of energy. I enjoyed myself as I answered students' questions and helped them seek out useful materials.

Then things would start to quiet down. On one such quiet day, I decided to see how the students were doing with their notes. I began with a student who was researching tuberculosis. "What happens when a person has tuberculosis?" I asked. She could not tell me one symptom of tuberculosis, although she had pages of notes. I moved on to a boy whose topic was alcoholism. All his notes were on drunk driving. "Why drunk driving?" I asked. "Are all drunk drivers alcoholics?" His astonishing answer made perfect sense to him. He had looked up alcoholism, or maybe it was alcohol, and everything he had found was about drunk driving, therefore he was copying down that information. Across the room sat a girl with a pile of books, but no notes. "What do I do now?" she wailed.

As I pondered that question, I began to realize that we had missed a crucial step in the research process. Students needed to know what they were looking for, and they needed to care. I began to look for strategies that would evoke this missing direction and ownership, presearches that could be done before what we traditionally think of as research. A good presearch would have two essential components: Students would begin their research from a base of knowledge. If they did not already possess enough background knowledge, they would acquire it before beginning their research. From their knowledge base, students would formulate research questions that interested them.

KWL

The KWL is probably the most widely known and commonly employed presearch. The K stands for what you already know about a topic, the W for what you want to learn, and the L for what you did learn. When students do have some prior knowledge of their topics, this can be a good place to start. I use a two-column printed form, but students can also fold a piece of paper in half. In the first column they write everything they already know about their topic. "Penguins live in very cold places." "Penguin fathers make good parents." In the second column, they write everything they would like know. The things they do know will usually lead to follow-up questions: "What things help penguins survive in cold places?" "How do penguins take care of their young?" I used to be tempted to reword their questions using scientific terms like *adaptation*, and *family structure*. Experience taught me that rewording a question takes away ownership; often a student no longer even understands the question or recognizes it as his.

Sometimes the questions for a specific type of report seem so obvious to us that we want to give them to students so they do not miss anything important. Everyone knows the questions that come with the ubiquitous animal report. That student trying to unravel the mystery of how penguins are able to live in extremely cold places is going to learn quite a bit about their "habitat." I believe she is going to dig deeper for information, and understand and remember more than a student who does not pursue his own questions. I will never forget the boy who wanted to know what a beaver's tail was made of. In the standard animal report this probably would have been part of a category called "physical description," and the researcher might never have gone into such detail with such enthusiasm.

The enthusiasm is there from the start with questions students have generated themselves, as researchers ask "I wonder why . . . ?" and "I wonder how . . . ?" They need to know the answers, and so their enthusiasm now extends to unlikely objects like indexes and specialized reference works that help them track down their information. They are engaged as they read. "I thought so," someone triumphantly announces. "Wow! I didn't know that," another declares. All this excitement is likely to make their final products genuinely interesting too.

When students sum up what they have learned at the end of the project, they will be proud of what they have accomplished.

Kinesthetic KWL

Here is an approach that gets active learners out of their seats and works well with small groups. Cut standard size paper in half. Give each group several pieces. If you have the time or inclination, the paper can represent a shape, like raindrops for a project on rain. The groups write something they know about a topic on each paper, for instance, "In some places it rains a lot, and in other places it rains very little." Groups toss their papers in the air and move around the room reading the comments of other groups until they find one that interests them. They write several follow-up questions for the comment they choose. For the above comment they might ask, "How do plants and animals adapt to lots of rain?" "What causes some areas to receive large amounts of rain?" When they finish with one comment, they may select another. Groups can choose to research one of the topics for which they developed questions, or they can select one "left over" by another group.

Instant Version

Peter Elbow's writing exercise, "Instant Version," can also serve as a presearch when students have some knowledge of their topics. Before they begin their research, they each write a sketch of the final product as though they knew everything. When they are uncertain about the facts, they can either guess or draw little boxes to indicate what they are leaving out. Elbow asserts that writing an "Instant Version" can "catapult you into a position of initiative and control so that you can use reading and research to check and revise your thinking actively, not passively just to find something to think." (Elbow 1981)

This strategy requires an adventurous teacher with a class that has caught that spirit of adventure. I would not try this on sixth graders, who tend to be literal and see things in black and white. Older students who have achieved some fluency in writing may find their interest levels raised considerably when they write an instant version. This is also a natural for gifted students.

Brainstorm, Read, Categorize

Remember those students taking notes on tuberculosis and alcoholism? No study of disease had preceded their assignments, so they lacked the framework for thinking about and making sense of their topics. Of course, they had some knowledge of disease. They had all been sick; they had all known people who were sick, sometimes quite seriously sick. They needed a presearch that would move them from their personal knowledge to the exploration of more complex background information.

Students begin the presearch by making individual lists of all the words that come to mind when they recall their own illnesses and those of relatives and friends. Some students also like to picture television shows or movies that revolve around hospitals and sick people. After they make their own lists, they contribute to a group list on an overhead transparency. These personal words are often intense: sad, death, pain, vomit, comforting. Their interest levels increase with these links to their own experiences.

Next, it's time to lengthen their lists with words that doctors, nurses and medical researchers might use when talking about disease. To help them do this, I distribute a ten-page encyclopedia article on disease and tell them they have ten minutes to read it. When the cries of protest die down, I explain that they will obviously not be reading every word. As they skim through the article, looking for useful words to add to their lists, they are to pay particular attention to the subtitles for each section because they indicate important categories of information. The words they choose should be those that help people think about disease, and they must understand each word and be able to define it. I announce when half their time is up and also give them a "two-minute warning."

We again add words from their individual lists to the group list, but now we have terms like *treatment, diagnosis, bacteria, lymphocytes, transfusion*. I ask if they are surprised they could learn so much in just ten minutes of skimming an article, and without copying word-for-word. Almost everybody is.

Finally, they put their words into categories. I define categorizing as grouping things by a common characteristic and giving that group a label. They practice categorizing themselves—boys, girls, people with glasses, etc. When they turn their attention to the word list, I find that some categories vary from class to class, but causes, symptoms, and treatments always emerge. I could have just given the students an assignment sheet requiring them to cover these things, but after the full period required for them to get there on their own, they really understand these words. They have a connection to them.

On the following day, students are required to find encyclopedia articles on their topics. These articles provide some needed background as students work to develop three good researchable questions about their topics. The encyclopedia will warn students away from questions that will not work. No sense asking what causes a disease if nobody's certain, but theories about possible causes might lead to interesting information. I then put yesterday's transparency on the overhead, and we review the categories for some good leads to framing questions. The article on their topic may also highlight some interesting areas they did not identify on the transparency. Finally, students must be warned not to pose questions that can be answered with a single sentence.

Somebody is still going to come up with a question such as, "Do you die from it?" Someone else will ask about cures when there are none. Knowing this, I always collect their questions and look them over. When there are problems, I work with the students to develop solid questions that interest them. It is a good idea to approve students' questions, no matter what presearch strategy you are using, and to insist that students get your approval again if they wish to change any questions.

This categorizing strategy works best when all the research topics fall into a single broad area. Reading generally about a subject like war or religion will clarify the major issues and characteristics that learners might explore when researching a specific war or religion.

Relax, Read, Reflect

Kuhlthau's (1994) work on the library research process provided the inspiration for this presearch. It is useful when students have little or no prior knowledge and their topics do not fall neatly in one category. Think back to Olivia, the girl who was researching Marian Anderson. She and her classmates were developing exhibits for a historical museum. They shared a common period, the Great Depression, but their topics were varied: the Dust Bowl, the Stock Market Crash, FDR, the CIO. Like Olivia, they had little familiarity with their topics when they began. Like her, they had chosen their topics because something in the initial brief explanation had appealed to them: people losing lots of money, workers engaging in sit-down strikes.

These students can acquire enough background to form good questions by reading brief overviews that highlight central issues and events related to their topics. I quickly discovered that the best overviews were usually not in the general encyclopedias that students were likely to resort to, but in reference sources with subjects as varied as the students' topics: African American history, biographies of women, environmental science, music, art, sports. It would have taken days to help everyone locate a useful source, to say nothing of the ensuing chaos and frustration. So I provide the overviews. Locating them initially was a lot of work; now I just refer to my records and assemble them the night before. If I find that two students will need the same volume, I make a photocopy.

Having avoided the chaos and frustration of a difficult search, I am ready to establish the relaxed mood that is crucial to this presearch. I want my students to enjoy this first exploration of their topic. "Look for things that interest and excite you," I tell them. "You are going to be spending a lot of time on this topic; you might as well find a way to have fun with it." They are to relax as they read, and that means no notetaking.

However, they must read carefully, looking for definitions, statistics, influential people, related events, surrounding controversies, opposing points of view. I leave this list on the overhead while they spend most of the period reading. During the final ten minutes, they make a list of five or six things that interested them about their topics. Usually, both their subject teacher and I read their lists. We write comments commending those who are off to a good start, and identify those who are struggling so that we can give them extra help the following day.

The goal of that next day is to develop three to five questions that will focus their research. Most will need the full period to do this. I encourage them to consider all their resources, not just the overviews, as they work on their questions. Some questions suggested by the overviews may prove unresearchable. Lengthy sources may cover some interesting areas not mentioned in the overviews. Many start with three questions, leaving room to add a question or two later when they know more about their topics. I begin the class with some examples of good and bad questions (see Chapter 4). Their teacher and I are busy for the rest of the period helping students, and we use the same procedure after class to review their questions.

Newspapers for a Background on Current Issues

If students will be researching issues as current as today's news, newspapers can help them understand and become interested in those issues. Small groups are initially assigned a broad topic like sewage treatment or world fisheries. They collect all the articles they can find for several weeks. At least once a week, they are given class time to discuss with other group members what they have been learning. Certain aspects of their topics will emerge as the most interesting. Groups can become fascinated by questions they would have rejected outright had they simply found them on a list of possible topics. A group may *need* to know whether it is dangerous to use sewage sludge as fertilizer. A visit to the library to check the periodical index, the Internet, and up-to-date books helps them determine if their questions are researchable.

Journal Writing

When students are allowed to research any topic of interest to them, it should be a wonderful opportunity, but it can just as easily turn into a nightmare. Very few students will know immediately what that interesting topic is, but structured journal writing can help them find it. A teacher can provide writing prompts for several days before topic selection is required. A good starter is, "Something I have always wondered about in (choose one of these subjects: nature, environment, science, technology, politics, world affairs, art, music) is. . . . " Another starter is, "Something I really care about or worry about is . . . so I think it would help me to know more about. . . . " When students insist they are drawing complete blanks, a stack of newspapers and magazines can help them zero in on areas of interest. On another day, they might visit the library to browse the shelves, then write about something that captures their attention.

As students find "their" topics, they can start to figure out exactly what they will need to know. They should develop specific research questions, and they may need to read some overview material. Since their topics could be anything, and school library media centers do not have information on everything, students must also do preliminary searches to prove that adequate resources are available. All of this information can be recorded in their journals.

COMPENSATE WHEN THERE IS NO PRESEARCH

Not every teacher will feel they have time for a presearch, but many will respond positively to your request for a little time at the beginning of an assignment. I have a mostly blank transparency ready for these situations. At the top, it says:

"If you don't know where you are going, how will you get there?

Begin your research by asking, What information am I looking for?"

If you are lucky enough to see the assignment before you see the students, you can anticipate possible difficulties. Let me give you an example. Mr. Byrd had put his assignment in my box. I read it through and found myself unable to answer the question on my transparency. I read it more carefully, and found there were three major areas of inquiry embedded in the second paragraph. When the class arrived, I was not surprised to find that they had fastened on the most exciting part of the assignment: designing a space probe. They were shocked when I insisted there was more. I directed them to read the second paragraph.

Some who had made preliminary sketches were saddened to find they would have to do research and take notes on the design of space probes. We need notes? asked one crestfallen girl. They were also to choose a destination and find out about conditions there. And they needed to learn about the kinds of research conducted by space probes. I had them identify sub-questions for the three major questions. That's a lot, someone sighed. I agreed. That was why they were going to spend a week in the library.

I kept the transparency on which I had written their research questions. It would be useful for keeping them focused. The next day, I checked to see if they were pursuing their questions. I asked how many had chosen a destination and learned something about it. The students who answered provided models for both the kinds of information needed, things like atmosphere and weather, and the places one might look for information, such as astronomy reference books and CD-ROMs.

Teachers often feel defensive when it becomes clear that students do not understand an assignment. We went over all of this in class, they will lament. It is important to assure them that it is perfectly normal for students to be confused at the start. Helping students clarify the purpose of their research will increase their chances of doing quality work.

You can and should go through this clarifying process even when you have not seen the assignment. Things will seem a bit murkier since you will be in the same state of confusion as many of your students. Failing all else, you can read the assignment together— if there is a written assignment. If all students have is a topic—for instance, the name of a president, you can fall back on that old faithful—what sorts of things would you like to know about a president?

THE GOAL: A PRESEARCH
FOR ALL RESEARCH ASSIGNMENTS

Persuading teachers to include a presearch is not an easy sell. It's not the way they learned to do research. They may already feel overwhelmed by the task of covering a seemingly ever-expanding curriculum. They may value the help you can provide with acknowledged research fundamentals like searching for resources and taking notes, but at first glance a presearch can seem like an extra, a frill. Sounds nice, they may say, but there just isn't time.

Allow yourself time to succeed with presearches. Find the more adventurous teachers and try a few of the strategies outlined here. Look for additional strategies and develop your own. Wait for word to spread about the benefits of a presearch. When students have a structure for examining their own knowledge of a topic and adding to that knowledge should it prove limited, they can develop solid research questions they understand and care about. When we provide time for a presearch, we communicate that thoughtfulness and reflection are to be vital parts of the research process.

REFERENCES

Elbow, Peter. 1981. *Writing with power: Techniques for mastering the writing process.* New York: Oxford University Press. 65.

Kuhlthau, Carol Collier. 1994. *Teaching the library research process.* Metuchen, NJ: Scarecrow Press. 71.

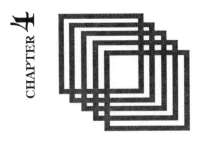

CHAPTER 4

Generating Questions

A Sense of Wonder

The unit began with a two-day presearch. On the third day, most students started searching for information. A few still sat dejectedly looking at their overview information one more time, or staring into space as if they expected salvation suddenly to appear before them. These were the students who still did not have approved questions. The science teacher sat beside one lost soul; the teacher-librarian talked with another. They both probed the students' background knowledge, trying to point them toward possible avenues of inquiry. "I just don't get this question business," one of the students sighed.

Over lunch, the two teachers asked themselves what they might do to help clarify the "question business." A social studies teacher and a special education aide agreed that many students seemed to struggle to find good questions. "What makes a 'good' question?" asked the band teacher. He listened, bemused, to a list of criteria (see Fig. 4.1), but he did not really understand until they gave him some examples of good questions. They believed they had just discovered something; their students would probably pose better questions if provided with outstanding examples.

Fig. 4.1. Criteria for Research Questions

- Based on knowledge of the topic

- Focus not too broad or too narrow

- Interesting to researcher

- Potentially interesting to others

- Feasible resources available to answer question

USE MODELS FOR
GENERATING QUESTIONS

I have always taught a mini-lesson before asking students to generate their own questions. Initially, I just presented examples that were too narrow or too broad. The class practiced posing good questions by fixing these bad ones. That is a good approach as far as it goes, but a substantial minority of students always had difficulty with the "question business." Over time, I became convinced that all students would find the task easier if presented with a model for posing solid research questions.

The Five W's and an H

The most well-known model for posing questions is undoubtedly the journalist's *who, what, when, where, why, and how*. It works best when applied to events and issues—the sorts of situations for which this model was originally designed. If students apply the five W's and an H to a historical event, such as the discovery of radium, they will usually come up with a fairly decent set of questions: "Who was involved in the discovery of radium?" "What is radium?" "When did the events leading up to the discovery of radium occur?" "How was radium discovered?" "Why was the discovery of radium important?" "Where . . . ?" And here we uncover a difficulty. As a sentence starter, "where" will probably lead to, "Where was radium discovered?" If a student is flexible enough to move "where" to the middle of the sentence, he might be able to ask, What equipment was used in the laboratory *where* radium was discovered? Literal students, a category that includes most sixth graders, will insist that this is a "what" question.

When teaching the five W's and an H, begin with topics that will yield good questions for all six sentence starters. Then move on to the type of problems encountered with the discovery of radium, and demonstrate how moving a word to the middle of a sentence can lead to a more interesting question. You may want students to practice developing questions while rearranging word order, but be careful to choose topics about which they already know something. Remember the first criterion for a research question in figure 4.1. To ask a question, they must know enough to know what they do not know. When students move on to their own topics, they need to use knowledge either recalled or acquired through a presearch.

It is important to present examples of bad questions. The most common problem is a focus so broad and undefined that almost any information on the topic could be counted as relevant. "Who was Chief Joseph?" "What was Prohibition?" When students are asked to describe the focus of a researcher answering these broad questions, they usually see the problem. One can also have too narrow a focus. "What was Babe Ruth's lifetime batting average?" "What percentage of women over 60 will develop breast cancer?" Requiring students to discard any question that can be answered in a sentence or two will help them avoid overly narrow questions. *When* and *where* are the words most likely to produce limited or trivial questions, and sometimes no amount of changing their positions in a sentence will overcome this problem. Let students know that not all six categories will always yield good questions. If they have one that is not working for them and they can convince you that it really is useless, allow them to eliminate it.

Question Stems

Question stems consist of several words used to begin a question. Stems are included in the inquiry performance tasks developed by the Minnesota Department of Children, Families and Learning. The first six stems in figure 4.2. are part of their performance task for framing research questions (Dalbotten 1997).

Fig. 4.2. Question Stems

- How do/does/did . . .

- What procedures or actions . . .

- What problems . . .

- What happens when . . .

- What is/was the role of . . . in . . .

- What is/was the difference between . . . and . . .

- What causes/caused . . .

- What are/were the effects/results of . . .

- How/why did . . . decide to . . .

- Who/what influenced . . . to . . .

- What is/was the relationship between . . . and . . .

- What are the competing sides . . .

- How does/did . . . change . . .

Stems do not leave as much up to the learner's imagination as the five W's and an H, but they are likely to produce more imaginative questions. They point students in directions that have often proved useful to researchers. Yet for all their precision, stems are also quite flexible; they can be applied to almost any subject matter. The stem "what problems . . . " can lead to "What problems did slaves face after the Civil War?" or "What problems occur when wetlands are developed?" or "What problems will a person with multiple sclerosis encounter?"

Present outstanding examples of questions to show students how to apply the stems. The question, "What were the differences between Herbert Hoover and Franklin Delano Roosevelt in the 1932 presidential election?" inspired a student to ask, "What were the differences between Langston Hughes and the African American writers who preceded him?" You will have to start by making up your own examples, but if you collect your students' best questions, you will soon have plenty to share. After sharing the examples, have students use the stems to develop as many questions as they can for their topic. Evaluating their questions in pairs or small groups helps students refine their questions and select the best ones to pursue.

Almost anyone can recite the five W's and an H, but it is a lot harder to remember question stems. List them on a handout that is always available to students.

Question Frames

Question stems are like launching pads that propel researchers into their questions; question frames are more like special lenses that allow them to examine a topic from different perspectives and pose questions based on what they see. Question frames are more abstract, and therefore more appropriate for older, advanced students. To examine a topic using a frame, one must have substantial background knowledge, so an extensive presearch is useful. Many possibilities exist for question frames; I find the four developed by Booth, Colomb and Williams (1995) the most useful. If you wish to examine additional frames, the Minnesota Department of Children, Families and Learning includes five different frames in their inquiry performance task for framing questions (Dalbotten 1997), and Tchudi (1987, 27–28) lists six frames in a section on "Lateral Thinking."

Fig. 4.3. Question Frames

- Parts and wholes
- History
- Similarities and differences
- Value or usefulness

The first frame is "parts and wholes." Students begin by identifying parts of their topic. Owen, a student studying management of salmon fisheries, asked these questions: "What are the roles of different levels of government (international, national, state, provincial) in fisheries management?" "What are the basic concerns of different types of fishers—sport, commercial, Native American?" "What concerns do environmentalists have about fisheries management?" Next, he considered the larger wholes that his topic was part of, and asked: "How does international politics affect fisheries management?" "What impact do other environmental issues, such as logging and water pollution, have on fisheries management?"

The second frame requires the researcher to trace the history of his topic. From this vantage point Owen found himself wondering: "How did fisheries management begin? How has fisheries management changed?" "How have changes in the salmon population affected fisheries management?" Next, he considered management of salmon fisheries as part of a larger history, and asked: "How have changes in the environmental movement impacted fisheries management?" "How have changes in fishing technology affected fisheries management?"

Booth, Colomb, and Williams call their third frame "categories and characteristics." I use the term *similarities and differences* to better distinguish this frame from "parts and wholes." Owen wanted to know: "What are the conflicts between various stakeholders and interest groups concerned about fisheries management?" "Do these groups have some common interests?" "How do these groups vary in their ability to affect the process?" Next, he considered his topic as part of a larger similar category and asked: "What are the similarities and differences between the management of salmon fisheries and the management of rockfish?"

"Determining value or usefulness," the fourth frame, highlights an area often overlooked in research. More than any other questions he had posed, Owen wanted to know the answers to these: "What is the likelihood that effective fisheries management can save the salmon?" "Are some management strategies more effective than others in protecting salmon?" "Are there negative consequences of fisheries management?"

Such a list provides many high quality questions from which to choose. Organizing the questions in a web may help show relationships between questions in different categories and thus make selection easier. Small groups can help by identifying the questions they would like answered. If the research will later be shared with the class, here is the promise of a curious audience.

Methodologies of Specific Disciplines

Within a specific area of study, certain types of questions are asked. Historians want to know about causes and effects of historical events; they look for patterns and recurrences of similar events. Anthropologists examine cultures by looking at such things as family structure, power structure, communication patterns, myths and legends. Horticulturists want to know . . . Ah, what do they want to know?

Reis and Renzulli (1992) point out, "Most teachers are not themselves well-versed in asking the right questions about specific fields of study. . . . " They suggest that we can promote creativity and involvement among highly gifted students engaged in independent research by enabling them to ask the sorts of questions routinely posed by researchers in a particular field of inquiry. To overcome the gaps in teachers' and librarians' knowledge, Reis and Renzulli (1992) propose that librarians help students locate books that present the methodology of a particular discipline. For me, and if demand justifies, this means adding such books to the collection or, when it does not, obtaining them through interlibrary loan.

This approach also works with students who are not gifted. A sixth-grade teacher wanted his heterogeneously-grouped students to research different cultures as part of an anthropology unit. He asked them to generate anthropological questions. They used their text to identify categories of information that interest anthropologists, and then they worked in small groups to brainstorm questions for each of the categories. His two classes were quite different, and their questions reflected these differences. The class with lower skill levels tended to ask about a culture's concrete things, for example, *what kind of gods do they have?* The more sophisticated class wanted to know about the values reflected in their culture's religion.

INCLUDE ASSESSMENT CHECKPOINTS

Teachers and teacher-librarians can and should evaluate whether students' questions meet the first two criteria for good questions (see Fig. 4.1), but only the students will know if they meet the third. When students assess their questions in small groups, they can also test how well they are doing with the fourth criterion. Working in a group can help students determine both whether their questions interest them and whether they will be of interest to others. If students cannot explain why they want to know the answers, they will probably not be able to interest anyone else in them. Having to present and assess their questions in groups helps motivate researchers.

Who has not heard a student, after several days of research, complain that there is simply nothing on his topic, or that the resources about his topic have nothing do with his questions? For many recurring units of study, your library is probably like a well-stocked trout pond, and the question of adequate resources will not be an issue. When students are pursuing independent projects or a teacher has decided to try something new, it is wise to ask students to do a preliminary search to see if their questions will meet the fifth criterion. Be clear before they start about exactly how many resources will be deemed "enough."

Coming up with good research questions is not easy; it is one of the hardest things we ask students to do. It takes practice to become a good questioner. You can help your students become more proficient by requiring them to reflect on the usefulness of their questions after they have completed their research (see Handout 4.1, p. 39).

VALUE STUDENTS' OWN INFORMATION NEEDS

All children are born curious, but unless their curiosity is affirmed and nurtured, it starts to die. The very first standard in the new *Information Literacy Standards for Student Learning* (AASL and AECT, 1998) declares that a student who is information literate "recognizes the need for information." Unfortunately, in many classrooms, when a student demonstrates a need for information by asking a question, that need will be ignored, because it does not fit the lesson plan or will slow down the covering of the curriculum. When only the teacher's questions are legitimate and they are "primarily asked to evaluate students and to manage the classroom, students will develop an aversion to questions and will fail to realize the power of questions" (Hunkins, 1989). Librarians must work with teachers to make their school a place where questions are valued.

Teachers As Models

Our local parks department asked the art teacher at my school if she would like to have her students work on a mural for our neighborhood swimming pool. She was excited at the prospect, but immediately recognized an information need. The theme was to be marine life; if the walls were not to be covered with generic fish, students would have to do some research.

The clever woman never called it "research." She simply sent small groups of students to the library to find out about aquatic life so they could choose the creature they wished to paint. Some needed to know exactly what a specific creature, such as a squid, looked like; others had identified a type—a really pretty fish or a weird one. All attacked this information quest with enthusiasm; they were in complete agreement with their teacher about a need for information. Months later, at the reopening of the pool, we all realized how much their research had contributed to the quality of their art work.

In addition to identifying information needs for students, teachers must recognize the information needs students identify on their own. When an eighth-grade science teacher took on a salmon-hatching project, she sent a steady stream of students to the library with questions about fish. It takes practice and flexibility for a teacher to respond to spontaneous questions from students. Some more formal techniques can facilitate the asking of questions.

QUESTION BULLETIN BOARDS

A question bulletin board is a place where students can post questions they would like answered. It works best if focused on the unit currently under study. Examples are "What we want to know about salmon" or "Questions we have about immigration." How the board is managed will depend on a teacher's style. Here are just a few possibilities. Students can be given extra credit for asking questions and for finding answers. Searching for answers can be an independent activity, or a teacher may send small groups to the library on a regular basis. The whole class can search for all or some of the answers. Students can post answers. Students can announce answers during an answer session that starts or ends the class. When more than one student answers the same question, the class can evaluate the answers for such things as completeness and clarity.

Credit is one way to motivate students to post questions on their own. A teacher should also post all unanswered questions that students pose during class. Assigning one student to record these questions makes it possible to note them without interrupting the flow of the class. Having special "question cards" makes questioning seem more official to students. These cards can also be used as exit slips on which students write down questions they were unable to ask during class. The teacher will want to answer immediately any questions that indicate confusion about the topic under study; the rest can be posted on the question board.

INFORMATION NEED PASSES

There will be times when students need and want to know the answer to a question as soon as possible. Information need passes (see Handout 4.3, p. 41) are for those times. "Don't sweat the small stuff," the saying goes. "Appreciate and affirm the small stuff," is what a teacher-librarian should think when a student comes to the library with an information need pass. Collaboratively planned research units may require much of our time and energy, but we must have something left over for the spontaneous, unplanned research that emerges when students' own questions are valued. It is not always easy, and students who need help may not always receive it immediately. The passes ensure that no one is overlooked or forgotten. Keep the unanswered ones so that you can reply to the teacher. Depending on your schedule, you may communicate a time when you can provide assistance or list some useful resources if you are going to be busy.

YOU SAY YOU WANT A REVOLUTION?

It takes time and practice for students to become effective generators of research questions. It also takes direction, which we provide when we present models for posing questions. And it takes thoughtfulness, the kind of thoughtfulness that emerges when students must assess their own questions. Finally, it takes a sense of wonder and spirit of inquiry that are nurtured in a school that values students' questions. When we provide all these things for our students they will begin to see themselves as responsible for their own learning—a revolutionary change.

REFERENCES

American Association of School Librarians (AASL) and Association for Educational Communications and Technology (AECT). 1998. *Information literacy standards for student learning*. Chicago: American Library Association. 9.

Booth, Wayne C., Gregory G. Colomb, and Joseph M. Williams. 1995. *The craft of research*. Chicago: University of Chicago Press. 40–41.

Dalbotten, Mary S. 1997. Inquiry graduation standards and performance assessment. Paper presented at the Eighth National Conference of the American Association of School Librarians, April, in Portland, OR.

Hunkins, Francis P. 1989. *Teaching thinking through effective questioning*. Norwood, MA: Christopher Gordon. 228.

Reis, Sally M., and Joseph S. Renzulli. 1992. The library media specialist's role in teaching study skills to high ability students. *School Library Media Quarterly* 21 (fall): 29–30.

Tchudi, Stephen. 1987. *The young learner's handbook*. New York: Scribner's. 27–28

HANDOUT 4.1

QUESTION STEMS

Name:_____

Topic:_____

See how many of these stems you can use to write a research question about your topic.

How do/does/did . . .

What procedures or actions . . .

What problems . . .

What happens when . . .

What is/was the role of . . . in . . .

What is/was the difference between . . .

What causes/ caused . . .

What are/were the effects/results of . . .

How/why did . . . decide to . . .

Who/what influenced . . . to . . .

What is/was the relationship between . . . and . . .

What are the competing sides . . .

How does/did . . . change . . .

HANDOUT
4.2

ASSESSING YOUR RESEARCH QUESTIONS

Name:_____

Topic:_____

What was your best question? Why did you like it?

What was your worst question? Why? (Skip this if you liked all your questions.)

Which questions led to the most interesting information? Why do you think they did?

Were there some questions for which you couldn't find answers? Why do you think you couldn't?

Knowing what you know now, are there some questions you would change? How would you change them?

Are there questions you wish you had asked? What are they, and why do you wish you had asked them?

What was the most useful thing you learned about developing good research questions that you can apply to your next project?

HANDOUT 4.3

INFORMATION NEED PASS

Date: _____

Time: _____

Student Name(s): _____

Teacher Signature: _____

My question is:

Librarian's comments:

CHAPTER 5

Planning

It's Really Great to Metacogitate

Mr. Wilson had just announced that the class would meet in the library tomorrow to begin research projects. Sean had a great topic, electric cars, and his questions were all about things he really wanted to know. So why did he feel so anxious? Tomorrow, everyone would be racing around the library looking for resources. That part was kind of fun, except when the bell rang and you still hadn't found anything. Suddenly, Sean found himself remembering the last project and his desperate race to finish his poster on time. Everything that had happened in between the frenzied beginning and the frantic end was a blur. What had he done during his week in the library? All he could remember was using an encyclopedia.

He heard Mr. Wilson asking the students to picture what they would be doing during the first period in the library. Sean figured he would probably start with the encyclopedias. Mr. Wilson wanted more than just one idea, though; he told them to imagine *everything* they might do tomorrow in the library. They were to get out paper, make lists, and then choose the best strategy for starting their research. Mr. Wilson had decided to try something new. His students were going to develop plans for their research at the start of each library period, and at the end of the period they would spend some time evaluating how well their plans had worked.

"We're going to try something new," Mr. Wilson told the class. "It's called metacognition."

WHAT IS METACOGNITION?

When students are aware of their own thinking, they are engaging in metacognition. They choose strategies deliberately, are aware of the steps they go through when solving a problem, and evaluate the success of their strategies after applying them. Metacognition becomes possible around the age of eleven, but some adults never develop the ability to metacogitate. If you were to ask them how they did something, they would not be able to tell you.

Fig. 5.1. Metacognition

1. Set goals

2. Identify strategies for achieving goals

3. Monitor effectiveness of strategies

4. Select alternative strategies when necessary

In school, many students follow instructions and complete a task without ever reflecting on what they are doing—it's just another hoop teachers want them to jump through. Asked later to do a similar task, they may not recall the strategies used earlier or realize that these strategies would be appropriate in a new situation. Like Sean, they may reflexively fall back on a tactic that has worked for them in the past. Perhaps it hasn't even worked all that well, but then they have never had to evaluate the usefulness of their strategies. They finished the project; they received a grade—isn't that all that is required?

When we want students to metacogitate, we must ask them to identify the strategies they will use to accomplish a goal, to monitor the effectiveness of their strategies, and to select other options when necessary. Planning is the research process step least likely to be included in an assignment. When there is a plan, it is often a list of due dates developed by the teacher for things like research questions, a list of sources, a minimum number of notes. Sometimes students are asked to develop a general plan at the start of their research in which they consider such things as search words and possible sources, but once developed, this plan is unlikely to be reconsidered or evaluated during students' research. In some cases, it may not even be consulted. If we want students to metacogitate, they must have daily practice.

USE JOURNALS TO PROMOTE METACOGNITION

The daily use of a journal is one of the best ways to build metacognition into a research project. Students develop plans for their research at the start of each library period and evaluate how well their plans worked at the end. This takes time, and that may be why this step is so often overlooked. Journals are most effective when used with an assignment of some length, at least a week and a half. Because planning and reflection are usually unfamiliar skills, it takes time for students to understand how to perform them effectively. The first time students use journals, they may not feel comfortable and confident until near the end of their research. Coaching by both the teacher-librarian and the classroom teacher will be necessary to help students develop their metacognitive abilities.

The first time I asked students to develop daily plans for their research, I simply had them write whatever came to mind on blank sheets of notebook paper. They wrote the evaluations of their plans on the back of the same sheets of paper. Students who were fluent writers, and/or extremely bright, did well with no more structure than this. I found that providing examples of successful plans to students who were struggling helped most of them improve over the course of their research. However, it would have been more efficient to structure their writing for them, rather than simply giving them blank sheets of paper where anything was possible. I decided to develop forms for both the plan and the evaluation before the next assignment that included a journal.

Booklets with Checklists and Forms

When students receive a booklet titled "My Research Journal," they are also being given a clear message. What they write inside this booklet is an important part of their research. That message is further reinforced when students are given time at the beginning and end of the period to write in their journals. The journal booklet contains side-by-side pages, enough for each day of their research, labeled "Research Plan" (see Handout 5.1, p. 53) and "Research Evaluation" (see Handout 5.2, p. 54).

In the research plan, students must begin by focusing on their questions, not just the topic. Kim, a student researching Korea, writes that she is asking, "What are Korean families like?" She says she is trying to find information about how children are raised and what mothers and fathers are expected to do. She wants to know what life is like for kids in Korea. She would also like to learn how marriages are arranged.

Next, Kim must identify the research process step that she is working on. To determine this, she looks at a page in the front of her journal called "Research Steps and Strategies Checklist" (see Handout 5.3, p. 55). She decides that she is now at step two, because she must plan her search. She hopes to begin step three by searching for information before the end of the period.

When asked her goal for the day, she declares she would like to locate at least three books that contain information on Korean families. To accomplish this, she will first brainstorm key words to use while searching, and then use the electronic catalog to find books that are in the school library. Kim adds that she loves the Internet, but doubts it will provide answers to her questions.

She identified her strategies by reviewing the ones listed under steps two and three on the "Research Steps and Strategies Checklist." I developed the checklist after too many bare-bones responses like "look for books" and "take notes." It reminds students of the many options open to them. Making a sensible choice is more important than their coming up with a possible strategy all by themselves. The basic checklist can be supplemented with a list of resources related to a specific subject, such as astronomy, or strategies geared to a specific type of final product, such as an oral report.

I also provide a "Feelings Checklist" to avoid such vague responses as "okay" in answer to the question, "How do you feel at this point in your research?" Words on the checklist include the following: *anxious, confident, interested, curious, frustrated, determined, jealous, discouraged, relieved, satisfied, happy, withdrawn, disappointed, confused, hopeful, uncertain,* and *enthusiastic.*

Not only does the checklist facilitate more precise responses, it also gives students permission to state that they are anxious or frustrated or confused. If the feelings are on the list, they must be acceptable. Students' responses about their feelings often provide me with the best indication of how well or poorly they are doing as well as assist me in targeting students who need extra help. Kim reports that she feels curious because she was born in Korea but was adopted by an American family as a baby.

For her evaluation at the end of the period, Kim must weave together several strands in describing how she used her strategies and the problems she encountered along the way. Then she must reach a conclusion about whether she accomplished her goal. It may seem like a lot to combine in a single response, but these three items do not work well as separate questions; they are related.

Because she has been asked to be specific in her description, Kim lists her search words: *Korea* and *families.* Because all the books she found from a subject search on Korea were checked out of her school's library, she requested several from other libraries on interlibrary loan. She did locate a book on families, but it did not have information on Korean families. Looking for a new strategy, she decided to search in the reference section but found no books on Korea. With the librarian's help, she discovered three geographical encyclopedias, two with good information about Korean families. She decides that, although she did not accomplish her goal of finding three good books, these two look helpful.

The most assertive and confident students will ask for help during the class period and persist even when the teacher-librarian is busy. The questions, "What would you like to ask the librarian?" and "What help can she give you?" are extremely valuable in ensuring that everyone else also gets individual help. Even Kim, who did ask for help during class, has a follow-up question. She wants to know if there are any CD-ROMs that might prove useful.

Kim responds to the "feelings" question by describing herself as disappointed that the books she wanted were not in the library. She adds that she feels anxious because she will not know if the books she has requested are useful until she sees them. Reading this, I make a note to check on Kim tomorrow to see how she is doing.

While Kim has taken real care with her journal responses, some students are likely to see the plan and evaluation forms as mere worksheets to be completed as quickly as possible. I insist that all writing be done in complete sentences, a full paragraph being the expectation for each response. If a student receives feedback that his or her plan must be constructed more thoughtfully, but the student still rushes through the process, I require daily approval by me or the teacher before that student can begin working on research.

Kim will do a plan and evaluation for every day she spends in the library. At the end of the project, she will complete a final evaluation (see Handout 5.4, p. 58). This allows her to reflect on the entire research process, and consider lessons learned, both good and bad, that she can apply to her next research project. Her assessment of her work, along with the assessments of her classmates, helps me identify areas of strength and weakness in my instructional program.

Blank Paper Journals

After a few experiences with journal booklets, students should become comfortable with planning and evaluating their research process. They may be ready to record their thoughts on blank notebook paper. This format works well with gifted students, and students accustomed to writing frequently in class. If journal writing is used in the presearch stage, as a strategy for generating research questions, it often seems natural to continue this type of writing throughout the entire research process.

Blank paper journals are less structured, but they should not be *un*structured. Daily writing prompts should be given. Certainly the question on the research plan form, "What do you hope to accomplish today and what strategies will you use to achieve your goal?" is a good beginning prompt. Some students will find it a useful daily starting point. The "Research Steps and Strategies Checklist" should be available for students to refer to, either as a handout, an overhead projection, or a poster. Other planning prompts might include the following: "What is the biggest information problem you still need to solve, and how will you try to solve it?" "Are you finding information on both sides of the issue, and what can you do to locate different views?"

Evaluation prompts ask students to describe their biggest success and/or failure. Writing a specific request for help from the librarian is another option. When the teacher-librarian and the classroom teacher have a solid collaborative relationship, they may want to develop prompts based on what they see happening as students do their research. Students might begin research on environmental topics with their minds already made up, only to discover strong opposing arguments. The teacher and teacher-librarian could present the prompt, "Are your initial ideas about the topic being challenged? How do you plan to deal with this?" This sort of prompt is likely to elicit a higher level of thinking than the questions on the "Research Plan" and "Research Evaluation."

Many additional useful prompts can be found in Julie Tallman's article on the I-Search Paper (Tallman 1995). In the I-Search method, originally developed by Ken Macrorie (1988), students' reflections on their searches for information are as important as their final products. Indeed, reflections are *part* of their final products because students use their journals to incorporate the stories of how they found their information and made sense of it.

EMPLOY OTHER APPROACHES TO PLANNING

Journals take time, both for students to write and for teacher-librarians to read and respond to; it would not be feasible to include them in every research project. Sometimes a less time-consuming format is needed.

Contingency Schematics

The concept of a contingency plan is a useful one for students. They must ask themselves what they will do if their chosen strategy does not work. A contingency plan can be laid out in the form of a diagram (see Fig. 5.2). On blank pieces of paper, students identify their goals for the period; they then list the strategies they will use to reach their goals. Alongside each strategy, they try to write an alternative in case the chosen strategy does not work. Again, the "Research Steps and Strategies Checklist" must be available. Visual students often prefer this approach to the more extensive writing required in a journal.

Fig. 5.2. Contingency Schematic

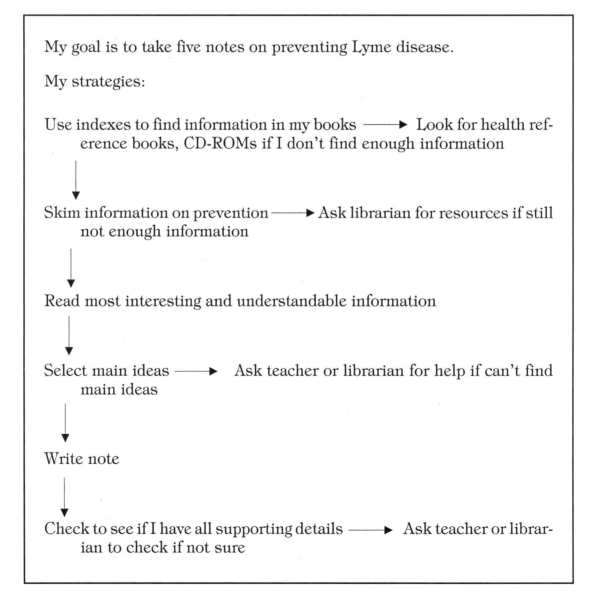

My goal is to take five notes on preventing Lyme disease.

My strategies:

Use indexes to find information in my books ⟶ Look for health reference books, CD-ROMs if I don't find enough information

Skim information on prevention ⟶ Ask librarian for resources if still not enough information

Read most interesting and understandable information

Select main ideas ⟶ Ask teacher or librarian for help if can't find main ideas

Write note

Check to see if I have all supporting details ⟶ Ask teacher or librarian to check if not sure

As students work on their research, my collaborative partner and I verify that students are actually using their plans. We collect the plans at the end of the first day to make sure that everyone is on the right track and offer suggestions to those who are not. After that, we collect the plans every other day.

Full Class Search Plans

Some planning and monitoring is better than none. When a formal planning step is not possible, classes can still brainstorm a list of possible sources before beginning their research. If this is done on a transparency, students can review the list each day to check which sources they have used. Briefly sharing stories of successes and difficulties will heighten their awareness. Even such a simplified approach to planning can prevent students like Sean, the boy who could not think of any source but an encyclopedia, from repeatedly reusing the single strategy they know.

Product Plans

Plans for final products present a dilemma. If students form plans too early in the research process, they may become so focused on the product that they slight the gathering of information. A student may ignore some useful facts because he does not believe he can incorporate them into a video presentation. Another student, who is trying to get fireworks to explode behind the titles of his multimedia presentation, may consider research an imposition that distracts him from his more important work. A young artist may spend all her time creating a beautifully designed poster that communicates nothing. On the other hand, a student without a plan for a poster may paste up tidbits of information and some pictures, and also communicate nothing. And who has not encountered the student who asks, "What script? What set? Just give me a camera; I'm ready." If the project is due tomorrow, there may be no alternative.

So it is a good idea to have students develop a plan for their final product—just not too soon. Midway through research is early enough. Students can figure out what information they need for their product and consider what they already have. A poster without pictures will be pretty dreary, so it may be time to begin looking for visuals. Although creating an actual hurricane or a reasonable facsimile is impossible, some pictures and charts could enhance a video presentation on the topic. Perhaps a student has become absorbed in one of the "sides" for a "compare and contrast paper" and needs to spend some time focusing on the other.

A production plan must also identify needed materials, and sources for these materials. One student may need to consider how and when he will gain access to a computer. Another may realize she will need to visit stores to assemble fabric samples for a display on fashion in the 1930s. A group planning a skit may divide the tasks, with one student finding background music, another locating costumes, and another making a butcher paper backdrop. Sometimes the issue may be as basic as collecting construction paper, scissors, and glue.

Finally, students will need a schedule. When will they find the fabric samples or locate the costumes? When will they complete a script, when revise, when rehearse? When will they develop a design, and when execute it?

Product planning can be incorporated into either of the journal formats, or done as a contingency schematic. If an assignment requires all students to produce the same kind of product, the class can brainstorm the elements that will be necessary for a successful production.

TEACH AND COACH THE PLANNING PROCESS

When students are first asked to plan their goals and strategies for a research project, the process is likely to seem confusing at best, and frightening at worst. They are not used to taking responsibility for their own learning. They will require instruction and support to succeed. That support will have to come from both the teacher-librarian and the classroom teacher. When a research assignment involves a planning step, the best collaborating teacher is one with a real interest in metacognition, one who will encourage and prod students to reflect and write.

Offer Models of Good Plans

The "Research Steps and Strategies Checklist" (Handout 5.3, p. 55) offers an outline of the research process, but it will not be sufficient to help most beginning students understand all they should be doing as they write in their journals or plot a contingency diagram. Students should first be offered some generic models, like the story of Kim's search for resources on Korean families or the diagram drawn up by the student who wanted to take notes about the prevention of Lyme disease (see Fig 5.2, p. 48). Collect well-executed student examples so that you have a variety dealing with different types of subjects, and different steps in the research process.

Students need models for different steps in the research process. They may become comfortable developing plans during the search phase but feel uncertain about what to write after they have gathered all their resources. As most students begin reading and taking notes, you may find one who has already developed a notetaking plan that can be shared with the class.

Start each class period by having some students share examples of success and frustration from the previous day. When one student relates how she located some helpful sources through a title keyword search, expect to see other students include this tactic in their plans. If another reports how he discovered some exciting reference sources on the environment, there will almost certainly be a crowd in the reference section that day. When a student presents a tale of woe, the whole class can brainstorm possible solutions to the problem; she is unlikely to be the only one who encountered it.

A review of student journals or plans after class will also highlight some commonly shared problems. In response to these, I might give a mini-lesson about the differences between searching on the catalog and searching on CD-ROMs, or the usefulness of indexes, or the use of the copyright date as an indication of currency. When I do this, I expect students to see me as a valuable resource, their journal plans declaring, "I will see the librarian for more help."

All of the various models, whether presented by teachers, librarians, or peers, will give students a more complex view of the research process and translate into more sophisticated plans. However, it takes time. Some students begin by writing only the sketchiest plans, because that's all they can envision. Others become good at planning only toward the end of that first experience. Such a student may need a second experience before feeling comfortable with developing a plan for research, monitoring that plan, and making adjustments. Metacognition is a higher-level thinking skill; it takes time and patience to develop.

Respond to Individual Journals

When there are 22 or 28 or 33 students in a class, often only the most assertive—or the most disruptive—will get individual help. A class period may go by in a blur, but later, when I read student journals, I am able to identify all the students who need assistance. By responding to individual journals, I am able to help everybody. My personal responses to their problems encourage students to keep writing in their journals, and to write truthfully. Because I have written notes to them, some will even start communicating directly to me and ask "Have you ever had this problem?" "Do you know what I should do now?"

I may also detect some students who are having difficulty with the planning process itself. Once having selected them for extra coaching, I will try to check on them as they write to see if I can offer assistance. As their coach, I try not to tell them what to do, but to ask questions to get them thinking.

When I sit down to read student journals, I find a time when the library is relatively quiet and my assistant is able to work with drop-ins. Otherwise, I must wait until students have gone home. I know I will most likely have to sprint to the catalog, or amble through the reference section, or open up an Internet connection, and I do not want to be interrupted.

Responding individually to journals is demanding work. With experience, I have learned some survival strategies. It is hard to respond to more than two classes at a time. If a teacher has four sections, I encourage scheduling just two at a time for research. If I can stagger the start of the classes, I am able to respond to students' journals on alternate days. I am less likely to tire if I am not working on another major research project at the same time. Presenting book talks and teaching students how to tell stories require a different sort of energy, and bring a nice balance to my life.

The first time I repeated using journals with the same teacher, and the same basic topics, I regretted not having taken any notes on the sources I had unearthed for the previous classes. Yes, I would recall, we had a hard time finding information on China's dowager empress last year. What were those reference books that had proved so helpful? I cut some narrow strips of tagboard. Every time I encountered a challenging topic like the empress, I wrote the topic at the top of the strip and listed places where information was available. I recorded only the less obvious sources, as when the empress turned up in a book on women rulers. Sometimes, I just noted that a search on the World Wide Web or magazine index CD-ROM proved helpful; if the search words were not clear-cut, I might list them, too.

Obviously, journal writing cannot be part of every research assignment. Since many teachers do not want to give up research time for student writing, this has never developed into a problem for me.

NURTURE INDEPENDENT LEARNERS

We want students to take charge of their own learning. What better way to teach them to do this than by asking them to plan for their research and monitor the effectiveness of their plans? We are teaching them to reflect upon and to learn from their successes. We are helping them to see problems as opportunities for uncovering new options and for learning new skills. Through planning, students learn that a big objective must be reached through a series of small steps. Include metacognition in your teaching of the research process, and you may be amazed by the depth of thinking and the growth that ultimately emerges.

And there's also the fun. It's a pleasure to feel competent and in control. I still treasure two students' comments from my very first experiment with research journals. One wrote, "I'm very proud of what I've done. It took a lot of work but it was fun." Another, considering what she had learned about research, declared, "It's tough, but it is also fun, challenging, and a great learning experience. I learned that the library is very large with all the facts it contains. It is fun to scurry around the library looking for books, magazines and encyclopedias. It's almost like the world is put inside one room, and it's there for you to explore. It takes patience" (Rankin 1988).

REFERENCES

Macrorie, Ken. 1988. *The I-search paper.* Rev. ed. of *Searching writing.* Portsmouth, NH: Boynton/Cook Heinemann.

Rankin, Virginia. 1988. One route to critical thinking. *School Library Journal* 34 (January): 29.

Tallman, Julie. 1995. Connecting writing and research through the I-search paper: A teaching partnership between the library program and the classroom. *Emergency Librarian* 23 (September–October): 22.

DAILY RESEARCH PLAN

Name:_____

Topic:_____

What research questions are you trying to answer? What kind of information are you looking for?

What step are you at in the research process?

What do you hope to accomplish today and what strategies will you use to achieve your goal?

How do you feel at this point in the process?

HANDOUT 5.2

DAILY RESEARCH EVALUATION

Name:_____

Topic:_____

Evaluate your work in the library today covering these points:

- Describe specifically and in detail how you used the strategies, for example, list titles of books you found, key words you used for searches, etc.

- Report on any problems encountered

- Decide whether you accomplished your goal

What would you like to ask the librarian? What help can he or she give you?

How do you feel after today's work in the library?

RESEARCH STEPS AND STRATEGIES CHECKLIST

HANDOUT 5.3

Name:_____

Topic:_____

STEP 1—PRESEARCH

Strategies

- Browse library collection

- Read encyclopedias and reference books for an overview of topic

- Recall what you already know about topic

- Write questions to guide your research

STEP 2—PLAN THE SEARCH

Strategies

- Brainstorm key words to use when searching

- List possible sources of information

- Consult with librarian and teacher to identify other sources of information

STEP 3—SEARCH FOR INFORMATION

Strategies

- Use electronic catalog to locate resources through subject, subject key word, and title key word searches

- Explore reference section using Dewey numbers related to your topic

- Search electronically using CD-ROMs and/or the Internet

- Locate magazine articles using the magazine index CD-ROM

- Use people as sources of information through interviews, surveys, letters

- Use indexes and tables of contents to locate useful information within books

Handout 5.3—*Continued*

STEP 4—SELECT INFORMATION

Strategies

- Evaluate whether resources match your reading level

- Determine if resources are up-to-date and reliable

- Decide if the information relates to your research questions

STEP 5—INTERPRET AND RECORD INFORMATION

Strategies

- Skim and scan to find information that answers your questions

- Read, view, or listen to sources

- Identify main ideas and supporting details

- Take summarized notes

- Classify and label notes

STEP 6—EVALUATE INFORMATION

Strategies

- Differentiate between fact and opinion

- Recognize points of view and biases

- Compare information from different sources and identify points of agreement and disagreement

- Review your notes to decide if you need additional information

In most cases, you will do Step 7, COMMUNICATE THE INFORMATION, and Step 8, EVALUATE THE RESEARCH PROCESS AND PRODUCT, after your library time is over. If you complete the first six steps before then, ask the librarian for the checklist for Steps 7 and 8.

Handout 5.3—*Continued*

STEP 7—COMMUNICATE THE INFORMATION

Strategies

- Organize your notes
- Use information in notes to determine important conclusions to be shared with others
- Write a summary statement or introduction for your research
- Compare and combine information from different sources
- Make an outline or web for final product
- Sketch a design for a visual display
- Create an original product
- Revise, edit, rehearse to insure a quality product

STEP 8—EVALUATE THE PROCESS AND PRODUCT

Strategies

- Determine if the assignment requirements were met
- Decide if research questions were answered
- Identify strengths and areas for improvement in applying the research process

HANDOUT 5.4

FINAL RESEARCH EVALUATION

Name:_____

Topic:_____

On the scale below, indicate how well you used your research time.

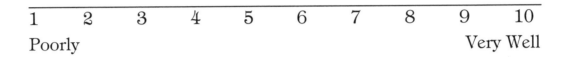

1	2	3	4	5	6	7	8	9	10
Poorly									Very Well

Do you feel you made the best possible use of the librarian? Why or why not?

What was the most useful thing you learned during this project about how to do research?

If you were starting this project again, what would you do differently?

How do you feel now that the project is over?

CHAPTER 6

Managing Time

Everybody's Problem

Mrs. Glass had been learning about performance assessment and had an exciting idea. She planned a year-long focus on the research process with her sixth graders. After a year of instruction, coaching, and practice, she would assess their ability to apply the process independently. When she sat down to consider this with the teacher-librarian, both were attempting something new. They began by identifying all the skills students would need to conduct a research inquiry on their own. They must be able to pose good questions, search effectively for resources, take summarized notes—the list lengthened. Mrs. Glass was lucky; since she taught language arts, social studies, and science to the same group of students, she would have enough time to fit all these skills into her program.

Time! Mrs. Glass and the teacher-librarian looked at each other. They were planning to give students eight hours in the library—spread over two or three days—to begin, carry out, and complete a research project. They pictured a possible scene in the library. Some students might feel overwhelmed by a variety of tasks all competing for their attention at the same time. Others might become absorbed in a single task and find themselves with a great stack of resources, only to discover that half the time had expired without their taking any notes. And still others would undoubtedly see several hours as an eternity and spend half of it socializing.

They would have to teach students to plan. Mrs. Glass and the teacher-librarian needed to define their goals and determine the strategies they would use to achieve them. Students, too, would need to break down the research process into a series of essential tasks. However, the best plans in the world would prove worthless if students failed to execute them because they managed their time poorly. Mrs. Glass added time management to the list of skills to teach.

Again, the two looked at each other. What exactly did time management mean? The school provided all students with a notebook for recording homework and assignment deadlines. This was generally considered helpful in teaching students to manage their time well. But the deadlines in their notebooks were imposed by teachers. If students were to be prepared to use completely unstructured time, they themselves would need to judge how much time should be allotted to each of the tasks required to complete their project.

THE RATIONAL PIECE—DESIGNING A TIME MANAGEMENT PLAN

The idea of planning for efficient use of time is foreign to most students. They are impulsive; they want to do what looks like fun; they want to do what their friends are doing. They live in the here and now. Just as they do not believe they will grow old someday, or die, so they often do not believe that a month or a week or even a few days will quickly pass, and their research assignment will be due. Their feelings about time and research are further complicated by a common perception that research is an addition to schoolwork, not an integral part of it. They complain that not only do they have to study for a big math test, do their weekly spelling and vocabulary work, and read the next chapter in their social studies text, but now they are also being asked to do research. So it is best to begin by making clear that time management is a real-life skill.

Introduce Students to Time Management

Most people have problems with time. If students reflect for a moment, they will realize that their parents often seem rushed and overextended. Most can probably remember an instance when a parent let them down because of other time demands—perhaps failing to bring home some needed item, or missing a performance at school. After asking students to consider the time management problems of others, I share some of my own difficulties with time management

Then I turn the spotlight on the students themselves. How many feel really busy? How many are always busy, working hard, but still falling behind? How many worry about all the things they have to do, but have trouble actually making themselves do them? How many put tasks off until the last minute and then finish in a frantic rush? How many put tasks off too long, and then cannot finish in time? After I finish polling them, students will often wish to add other problems.

Once they realize that everyone has problems with time—their parents, their teachers, their classmates—students' interest in time management techniques increases. You can extend the real-life connection by assuring them that they will not focus solely on school work as they learn these techniques, but they will also consider their family obligations, recreational needs, and anything else that places claims on their time. If they manage their time well they should be able to do the things they need to do, plus the things they want to do. If they do only the things they need to do, life may seem boring and empty of fun. If they do just what they want to do, they will probably end up disappointing a lot of people—a friend they failed to keep a promise to, a teacher who had expected an excellent project, a parent who believed them when they said they would try harder. Good time management should help them achieve a balance in their lives.

Teach a Planning Technique

Planning and time management dovetail nicely. The goals and strategies in a student's research plan provide the raw material for time management. Once the tasks involved in a research project have been identified, students can begin to decide how to allot their time. The metacognitive methods central to planning for research will also be applied to time management. Students will set goals for time use, identify strategies that will help them use their time well, monitor their efficiency, and choose alternative strategies when necessary (see fig. 5.1, p. 44). Several of the steps needed to develop a time management plan will seem very familiar (see fig. 6.1).

Fig. 6.1. Steps in Developing a Time Management Plan

1. Imagine your primary goal, your desired result

2. Identify all the tasks you must perform to reach your result

3. Organize tasks in a sequence—which tasks must be completed before others can be started?

4. Estimate total time available by considering assignment deadlines, and other demands on time

5. Estimate amount of time needed for each task

6. Develop a schedule for completing tasks

7. Determine when (and possibly where) each task will be carried out

8. Make a contingency plan for finding "extra time" when there are problems like:

    • unanticipated tasks

    • underestimating time needed for a task

9. Implement your plan

10. Monitor how well your plan is working, and make adjustments if needed

Let's follow one student as she develops her plan. Elizabeth always turned in her projects on time, but they usually looked as if they had been patched together at the last minute and then trampled on by a herd of elephants. Elizabeth was introduced to time management before the final research project of the year. When asked to envision her desired result, she decided that she wanted to finish her project before the deadline—and it was going to be neat and well organized.

Her teacher, Ms. Rico, had already identified the major tasks in the project—generating questions, finding sources, taking notes—through a calendar of ongoing deadlines. Using the "Research Steps and Strategies Checklist" (see Handout 5.3, pp. 55–57), Elizabeth was able to come up with most of the necessary sub-tasks. Since she always visited the public library when doing research, she added that to her list. Her teacher's deadlines made the sequencing easy. Still, Elizabeth knew her sequence would differ from many others because she liked to read quite a bit about her topic before taking any notes.

Elizabeth had a month to complete her project. It sounded like a lot of time, but she lived in a small apartment with her mother and six-year-old brother, and she was often called upon to baby-sit. It was impossible to get much work done while taking care of her brother. She was going to lose a whole weekend for soccer playoffs. She also needed to do some extra credit work to bring up her grade in science. Ms. Rico was giving them two weeks in the library for research, plus some class time for creating their displays. Once Elizabeth had calculated how much time she had available for this project, she knew she would have to work hard to meet her goal.

She determined that she would not waste a single minute of her class time in the library. Since working at home was often difficult, Elizabeth needed to figure out some additional times and places for working on her project. She decided to use her lunch time; after eating, she would retreat to a quiet corner of the library. She planned to do this for all four weeks of the project. This gave her twenty extra minutes each day. If this was not enough, she would start going to the homework room for an hour after school.

When the class began their research, Ms. Rico noticed that Elizabeth always started working before the bell rang. Sometimes she had to ask Elizabeth to put down her reading or notes to attend to a mini-lesson. She easily met all the early deadlines; it was not until they returned to the classroom that Elizabeth ran into trouble. She had seriously underestimated the amount of time needed to put together a visual display, and she had not realized that she would need to learn how to use a database to create graphs. She became a regular attendee at homework room. When she finished her project two days early, she decided to use the extra time to improve it, and ended up replacing some of her graphs with more effective ones.

Ms. Rico, accustomed to Elizabeth's usual slovenly approach, was astonished. Her display was well thought out; it told a powerful story with solid facts and strong feelings. It wasn't just neat; it was beautiful.

Evaluating her work at the end of the project, Elizabeth concluded that the most useful thing she had learned was to figure out how much time she had available. Without a time management plan, she would probably have found herself behind after the soccer weekend. Selecting when and where she would spend the time devoted to her project, plus identifying where she would find "extra" time if she needed it, ensured her success.

Elizabeth was lucky to be working on a well-structured assignment with a calendar of deadlines. Knowing when she had to complete each major task gave Elizabeth a model for allotting time during a research project. It would have been much harder for her to develop a schedule had she needed to determine all the deadlines except the final one. Since journals had been required for her two previous research projects, she was comfortable with planning. Her journal experience had also taught her how easy it was to underestimate the time needed to complete a task.

Some of Elizabeth's classmates had more difficulties. A few were very generous in their estimates of the time needed for each task; they found they would need six weeks instead of the allotted four. Developing a reasonable schedule was a much more challenging task for them as they struggled to pare down the time they would actually spend on each task. Others grossly underestimated the time needed for production tasks that occurred late in the project; some of these students worked nonstop the last few days, and a few turned in their displays late. Some students did not realistically take account of all the other demands on their time. Those who had good contingency plans were able to find the extra time they needed; those who did not either missed things like athletic practices or failed to meet the final deadline.

All in all, some valuable lessons were learned, and most students believed they would do a better job managing their time in the future. When the project was over, Ms. Rico decided that next year she would introduce time management earlier and during an assignment of shorter duration.

Apply Thinking Skills to Time Management

When students have had an opportunity to practice the thinking skills of problem solving (see Fig. 11.6, p. 137) and decision making (see Fig. 11.7, p. 137), they may find one or both of these skills useful in developing their time management plan. Hector, an extremely busy student, defines his problem as having too many demands on his time. He then identifies some possible options. He could eliminate one of his activities for a few weeks, perhaps art club or tennis practice. He could cut back on recreation, spending less time at the community center or in front of the television. He could pay his brother to do his paper route. He could beg his mom to excuse him from some chores for a limited time, as long as he proves he is spending the time on schoolwork. After he evaluates the plusses and minuses of each option, Hector is ready to choose the one that looks best. If his chosen option does not work well, he knows he still has others to consider.

Facilitate Student Sharing of Time Management Techniques

Some students will already have some techniques for managing their time. Others will add personal embellishments to the basic strategies for developing a time management plan. These students should have the opportunity to share their methods with classmates who have never managed their time, or who have always had their time managed for them by parents and teachers. Just as students will be reassured to learn that they are not alone in their difficulties with time, they may discover new possibilities when they realize that time management isn't just a "grown-up thing."

Student suggestions are likely to be listened to by peers. And they will probably come up with some techniques that would never occur to adults. One may announce that he has compared how well he works after school with how well he works after dinner. He did this by keeping a log of how long it took him to complete similar tasks, such as math problems or studying vocabulary, at both times of day. Two others might reveal that they helped each other meet deadlines by regularly checking on each other; neither one wanted to fail in the other's eyes. Another extremely busy student may declare that she always schedules some time for doing nothing. And another . . . Well, who knows? You and your students won't know until you ask.

THE AFFECTIVE PIECE—DEALING WITH PROCRASTINATION

Everyone procrastinates, but the ways in which individuals procrastinate, and their reasons, often vary. Some students have trouble starting a project; others falter at the end. Many put off tasks they do not find interesting, choosing to put their energy into assignments they enjoy. Others find the path blocked by a fear of failure. They do not expect to succeed, so what is the point of even starting? And procrastination can offer a great excuse for poor quality work—I know it's not very good; I did it at the last minute.

Life lived in a crisis mode can also have its rewards. While everyone else is working on research, a procrastinator has "free time" to socialize with other procrastinators or, maybe, to retreat to read a science fiction novel. At the end, there is the excitement of trying to pull everything together, probably in the company of friends who have also put things off until the last minute. There can be an almost festive atmosphere as everyone works side by side. It may also be necessary, even routine, to call in the troops. A parent is enlisted to make a frantic, last minute trip to the public library, where the reference librarian can be counted on to shift into high gear to deal with the emergency.

Cures for procrastination will vary with the cause. Some students may need strategies to make boring projects more interesting. Others may be able to overcome a fear of failure if presented with options for obtaining help. Still others may find that frequent rewards along the way can replace the thrill of a photo finish.

Overcome a Lack of Interest

Not every research assignment will be interesting to every student. Different types of assignments are likely to be interesting to different types of students. Students need coping strategies when they are working in a discipline or have drawn a topic that arouses not the slightest bit of curiosity in them.

Personalize a Topic

Students can personalize topics by relating them to their own lives. Lucas had been looking forward to researching Switzerland for his geography project, so he was not pleased when his teacher insisted on a lottery for countries. Lucas was even less pleased when he drew Sudan. After two days of protesting that Sudan was "boring" and "dumb," he allowed himself to be lured into posing a personal question. He asked, "How would my life be different if I lived in Sudan?" After one day of reading, he had concluded that the answer would depend on the religious and ethnic group to which he belonged. Now he found himself wondering which group he would prefer. Maybe he would want to join the group with the most power, but maybe he would like to be a "freedom fighter." He would have to keep researching before he could make a decision, but when he was finished he knew he would have an interesting story to tell.

Finding a personal source of information can also lead to heightened interest in a topic. Kyoko found her reading on diabetes boring and confusing until she interviewed her math teacher, who was a diabetic. Not only did her reading now make more sense, it also led her to so many new questions that she scheduled a second interview.

Similarly, Ira was convinced he had absolutely no interest in learning how fish were canned until he let himself be persuaded to call a cannery. He quickly discovered that most people love to talk about their jobs. By the time he hung up, he was fascinated, and eager to receive the information the manager had promised to send in the mail. He checked the encyclopedia to confirm that its account squared with what he had just heard. Then he planned to search for magazine articles about the problems faced by canneries.

Make Up for a Missing or Unsuccessful Presearch

One of the major purposes of a presearch is to motivate students. Unfortunately, not all assignments include a presearch. If someone is so alienated that he or she will not do any research, having that student do a presearch may be the most productive approach. Students often lack interest in topics about which they know little or nothing. The problem may be compounded if they possess misinformation or prejudices. The remedy may be as simple as having the student perform the "Relax, Read, Reflect" presearch (see Chapter 3). Once he or she acquires some background knowledge, and poses some questions based on that knowledge, interest should increase.

Sometimes a student has the opposite problem and feels that he or she already knows everything about a topic. An "Instant Version" presearch requires the know-it-all to write down all the known facts (see Chapter 3). While writing, these students may discover that there are some things they do not know. Even if they still believe they know everything, the task of verifying their preconceptions usually heightens interest.

Adjust Topics for High Risk, Low Skills Students

When a class must choose research topics from a set list, a student with low skills may end up choosing one of the most challenging topics. Faced with sources he cannot read, and concepts he cannot understand, such a student is doomed to failure. The special education teacher, the Title One teacher, and the classroom teacher can all identify students with poor skills before a research project begins. These students should be allowed to privately pre-select their topics from an abbreviated list of less challenging ones. Concrete topics, as opposed to more abstract ones, are most likely to capture the interest of students with low skills.

Every middle school seems to have some classes where almost all the students are below grade level in reading, writing, and thinking skills. A list of almost exclusively concrete topics may make the difference in whether the class as a whole becomes excited about a research project. A class that would struggle if asked to research such topics as "the Harlem Renaissance," or "the Scopes monkey trial," or "the first 100 days of the New Deal" will thoroughly enjoy learning about the airplanes, comics, artists, and sports stars of the 1920s and 1930s.

Use Rewards

When no amount of personalizing, presearching, or pre-selecting will make a topic interesting to a student, it's time to present the strategy of extrinsic rewards. Students can reward themselves for doing something they do not want to do. An hour of serious notetaking might earn a diligent researcher fifteen minutes of shooting hoops. Parents can also be enlisted. If a student promises to meet all deadlines in a research project, her parents can provide a predetermined and much desired reward—a trip to the movies or a week without dish washing—every time she succeeds. "Dressing up" the task itself works for some students. Notes can be taken either with colored pens or on colored cards. A desk at home can be painted an outrageous pattern with bright colors to lure a young learner to work.

Building in rewards all through a project may also reform the students who actually enjoy the frantic rush at the end.

Overcome Fear of Failure with Options for Help

I have discovered that students who have had little success with research assignments in the past are often the ones least likely to ask for help, no matter how desperately they may need it (Rankin 1992). They believe that if they ask for help—from their teacher, the teacher-librarian, or their parents—they are unlikely to receive it. Coaching them during research requires communicating that you care, that you expect them to succeed, and that you are willing to help.

Students who fear failure may sometimes want to ask for help but have no idea where to turn. Good coaching should include increasing their awareness of the options available for obtaining help.

Provide Non-Threatening Ways to Ask for Help

Successful students want to keep on succeeding, and they see no shame in asking for help when they require it. Failing students need to learn that it is okay to ask for help. Even when they understand this, they may feel embarrassed to ask publicly, so I like to provide some less obvious ways to ask for help. Journals, because they are read only by the teacher-librarian and perhaps the classroom teacher, are the most private way to request assistance (see Chapter 5).

When a class is not keeping journals, "exit slips" provide an alternative way to apply for help in writing. They are simply small sheets of paper, blank except for the title "Exit Slip" at the top. Students turn them in at the end of class, and they may contain a question about content or a request for help with the process. While the act of turning in a slip is public, the nature of a student's need remains private.

Supply Orderly After-School Work Spaces

More and more students struggle to complete assignments because they do not have a quiet, orderly workplace at home. Some of them can be found trying to finish assignments in the library media center both before and after school. All these students may require is a relatively quiet corner and occasional help from the teacher-librarian. Others need the more disciplined atmosphere of a "homework room." Typically, a homework room is open for an hour or two after school to provide assistance from teachers or volunteers in a serious, work-oriented environment.

Many community organizations also offer after-school work spaces. Public libraries often have a homework help desk and conference rooms that can be reserved for study. Youth groups like the Boys and Girls Clubs, and the "Y" may provide study spaces or programs. And don't forget the community center. Do some research on available work spaces and post a list of all the places where students can work after school.

Recruit Volunteer Help for Struggling Students

Some students will be more likely to succeed if provided with consistent, one-on-one support. As more and more women find it necessary to work, the available supply of parent volunteers has dwindled, but people willing and able to volunteer are still out there. Senior centers are frequently an untapped source of volunteer help. Businesses are increasingly likely to give employees time off to volunteer in schools. High school students can often fulfill a community service requirement by tutoring at a nearby middle school.

Then there are the middle school students themselves. Peer tutoring programs can work. They are relatively easy to supervise since both tutors and tutees are on-site. Students are likely to listen to peers who know what they are going through and who may have experienced some of the same difficulties themselves.

I try to connect with volunteers by notifying them of major research projects, clarifying assignment requirements, giving pointers on how to coach information skills, and communicating when students are in danger of missing deadlines. I keep a list of all tutors and tutees so I will know whom to contact when a student is having difficulties and could use extra help. Unless a tutor is aware of an assignment or a problem, he or she will not be able to provide that help.

Partner with Special Education Teachers

I have always found that special education teachers make great collaborative partners because it is their goal to work with others to help their students succeed. They are ready, willing, and eager to work with any teacher-librarian who shares this goal. I notify the special education teachers about upcoming research projects that will involve their students. After reviewing the assignment and assessment criteria, they can suggest any needed modifications—pre-selection of topics, fewer note cards or sources, an alternative presentation format. If they have a clear understanding of the assessment criteria, they will be better equipped to help special needs students meet those criteria.

I also update special education teachers during the research. I want them to be aware of students who are having difficulties, or missing deadlines, so that they can offer extra help. When time management plans are used, special education teachers can check them regularly to monitor students' progress. Since time management plans are often not used, special education teachers may want to teach their students how to design and use them.

Just as it is wise for a teacher-librarian to have a list of tutors and tutees, so also a list of all special needs students can prove invaluable.

Recognize the Special Worries of the Gifted Perfectionist

Students with poor skills are not the only ones who fear failure. Sometimes extremely bright students set impossibly high standards for themselves. They know they have no chance of meeting these standards, so they see no point in even trying. They need help in coming up with realistic standards and recognizing that there is no shame in having them. These students need encouragement, but most of all they need honesty. Only praiseworthy work should be praised. When I work with gifted perfectionists, I try to have realistic standards, too; these students are often the most difficult procrastinators to help. Perseverance will be needed.

The Teacher-Librarian's Role
in Preventing Failure

If one student fails to successfully complete a research project, that is one student too many for me. I consider any failure a blot on my record, so I am willing to go to great lengths to help my students succeed. When I see a student having trouble, I offer help, and then keep checking to see if the problem continues. When I help students, I try to communicate that I have the utmost faith in their ability to do research and do it well—if only they will try. I am their number one cheerleader. This can be crucial. One of the reasons Elizabeth, the girl with the excellent time management plan, succeeded was because I told her every day that I knew she could. I applauded every deadline met, and every attempt at neatness and order.

I use periodic process assessments to identify struggling students. When my coaching will not be sufficient, I look for someone else who can be of aid—a tutor, the special education teacher, the homework room supervisor, or perhaps a parent—and contact that person. When talking to parents of a struggling student, I try to elicit pointers that might help me succeed with their child. In exchange, I try to clarify the assignment so that they can help, too. My message to parents is not one of complaint; I am trying to enlist their assistance, because I know they care about their child.

I remind students that they can come to me for extra help—before school, after school, or during lunch. I repeat this message so often that they know I mean it. Because I sometimes have meetings or other conflicts, some students will actually schedule help time with me. As the year progresses, I acquire "regular customers" who count on me to look over their notes or review a first draft.

BE REALISTIC

It can be hard to persuade teachers to build instruction in time management into a research assignment. Ironically, they may feel there simply is not enough time for something that comes lower on their list of priorities than more obvious information skills such as notetaking or searching for resources. Only teachers like Mrs. Glass, who are interested in performance assessment, are likely to see time management as a crucial skill. While teacher-librarians may not have many opportunities to formally teach the technique of developing a time management plan, they can certainly present it informally to individual students with a need and an interest.

There will be more opportunities to implement the methods for dealing with procrastination. The strategies for overcoming lack of interest can be worked into mini-lessons at the start of class. The strategies for overcoming fear of failure will primarily require behind-the-scenes work by the teacher-librarian. Remember, most big problems are solved one step at a time.

REFERENCES

Rankin, Virginia. 1992. A wonderful idea for the library resource center: Piagetian theories applied to library research. *Emergency Librarian* 20 (November–December): 30.

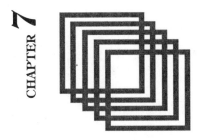

CHAPTER 7

Searching for Information

Location, Location, Location

"Oh no," Mario sighed, "this library has no books about George Washington."

A few minutes later, the librarian glanced at the OPAC (on-line public access catalog) as she passed; the search words on the screen read, "George Washington." She called out, inquiring if anyone needed information on George Washington, but the student had apparently departed. No chance to remind him or her that last names come first when searching for information about a person. The next screen, also abandoned, showed the search words *spruce trees*. When she asked if anyone wanted information on spruce trees, Noah's head appeared above a sports magazine. He informed her that the library did not have any information on spruce trees. With a little coaching on broadening his search, he soon had several books on trees that included sections on the spruce.

A wail of distress brought the librarian back to the OPAC terminals. Kate was complaining that all the books on thermodynamics had disappeared from the catalog. When she had searched two days ago, there had been eight, all of them in high school libraries. She had brought her research partner, Justine, to help her fill out the interlibrary loan forms. Now the books were mysteriously gone. Kate knew this had happened to her because she wasn't good with computers. Justine remained calm, scanning the screen for clues, and down at the bottom she found one. They could press "F5" to change libraries. Sure enough, this command brought up the missing high school books.

"Great problem solving, Justine," complimented the librarian, who had been standing silently behind them. "Our catalog software was just updated. Now we are able to limit a search to just the books in our own library, instead of searching for all the books in all the libraries in the district. F5 is the key that allows you to switch back and forth between these two kinds of searches."

WHAT SHOULD WE TEACH IN AN AGE OF TECHNOLOGY AND CHANGE?

Technology has transformed the process of searching for information. In the past, students might use the card catalog, but few claimed any fondness for it. Some did their best to avoid using it. Now, many students are eager to use an OPAC simply because they are eager to use a computer of any sort. That's the good news. The bad news is that they may see the computer as magical, and have complete faith in its ability to figure out exactly what they want. If they do not get results from their first search, they assume there is no information on their topic. Trying another search word or checking their spelling would never occur to them.

Many of the mistakes that students make on the OPAC are the same old ones they made using the card catalog. However, it is now easier to spot their mistakes because searches are often temporarily preserved on the computer screen. An open catalog drawer rarely revealed any clues. Sometimes you can find a confused student and help him or her right then. Sometimes you must make a note to try dealing with a common mistake through instruction or a handout or a poster.

Not all students are comfortable using computers; some try to avoid the OPAC the way students formerly avoided the card catalog. They are likely to blame their searching failures on their relationship with the hardware. "I'm just not good at computers," a student will sigh when an hour of searching the Web has yielded over 400 results, none of which appears to have anything to do with his or her topic.

Then there is the ever-changing software. The OPAC may look the same from year to year, but it keeps acquiring new features. It can be difficult and often impossible to make sure everyone is aware of, let alone knows how to use, really helpful additions such as title and subject keyword searching. CD-ROM references sometimes change so much that they bear little resemblance to the previous edition. Yet annual revisions seem glacially slow when one considers the Internet; there change is a daily occurrence.

We used to be able to teach students the way the card catalog worked and be pretty sure they could go to almost any other library and know what they were doing. The biggest surprise might be finding author, title, and subject cards all inter-filed. Now OPAC software can vary from school to school and from school to public library. Strategies that are useful for searching with an OPAC, like broadening a search, are often counterproductive on the Internet. Only the boldest crystal ball gazer would dare to predict the changes that may occur in electronic searching in the next decade.

How can we best equip our students to deal with the ever-present variety and inevitable change that electronic searching has produced?

A Problem-Solving Process

Students must be able to confront unfamiliar OPAC software, Web search engines, and CD-ROM resources and figure out how to use them effectively. Overconfident students, who trust the computer to produce results magically, need a problem-solving process that slows them down and causes them to reflect on their search. Students who are uncomfortable with computers need the reassurance that if they follow the steps in this process, they are likely to have success.

Handout 7.1, p. 82, guides students through the search process. Students begin with such queries as "What are my questions?" "What do I need to know?" Reviewing their questions helps them identify the narrowest and most specific search words. Then students are reminded that they may need to broaden their searches to find information. They complete the task of finding search words by looking for synonyms. By using a problem-solving approach, students come to understand that each step in the search process presents different options and that they must make choices. What search words do my questions suggest? Which type of search words may prove most useful—broader or narrower?

The next reflection point involves considering the type of information needed: a brief overview, a short answer to a simple question, in-depth information, data, opinions. It makes no sense to use the OPAC to find a whole book on Abraham Lincoln if I only need to know the years of his presidency. Using a CD-ROM encyclopedia will be much more efficient.

Therefore, it is crucial that students review the choices they have when it comes to search tools. The basic choices on the problem-solving handout—OPAC, magazine index, CD-ROMs, World Wide Web—can be expanded with an additional handout. This can be tailored to a specific assignment by listing relevant CD-ROMs and Web sites. Most students have a preferred starting place for searches, but now the process worksheet and additional handout remind them that they have other options. When they have gleaned everything possible (or perhaps nothing at all) from their favorite search tools, they have someplace else to go.

The next step in the process reminds students that there are many different modes of searching, and that different tools provide different search modes. Handout 7.1 may look like a worksheet that can be filled out at a desk. However, at this point in the process, a student will have to be sitting at a computer to determine which types of searching are possible using a specific tool—subject, author, title, keyword, Boolean, full text, or call number. They may also have to explore the help options to find out more about how a search tool works. Perhaps the on-screen directions on the OPAC mention keyword searching, or the magazine index CD-ROM places subject searching in a pull-down menu, or the help feature on a CD-ROM encyclopedia clarifies Boolean searching.

Of course, these modes of searching will only make sense if students have already been exposed to them. I use mini-lessons at the start of each library research period to explain the searches they may not have encountered, such as call number searches. It's also worth reviewing and reviewing and reviewing Boolean searches; student examples of successes using "and" "or" and "not" are likely to have the most impact. A unit where students rotate daily to different stations can expose them to a variety of different tools and types of searching, but there should always be a content-related purpose to their searches.

When students begin to use the problem-solving process for electronic searches, my goal is to increase their awareness of their options. It is not crucial that they immediately choose the most appropriate search tool or type of search. They will only become proficient at doing this through experience.

Rules for Searching

A problem-solving process is necessary for effective searching, but it is often not sufficient. A student can be thwarted by something as simple as a misspelled word if she never thinks to check her spelling. Another may fail to find resources if he does not use plurals on the OPAC. Yet another may be overwhelmed by the number of results that come from a Web search she should have narrowed with a Boolean "not."

Here is where librarians must be careful. Students, at least most students, do not think like us. They are not fascinated by all the ifs, ands, and buts of searching. If something will help them right now, they want to know about it, but they do not care about the theory of information science. Yet they need to know some of the rules and wrinkles of searching that will increase their successes.

When designing instruction in this area, I try to follow the KISS principle: Keep It Simple, Sweetheart. The ideal is to find an individual student with a problem and teach the needed rule or strategy right then. Since that's not always possible, I also use posters and handouts, keeping them brief, no longer than a single page for a handout. That means many things must be left out. What you include in a handout should be determined by the sorts of problems students in your particular school seem most likely to encounter.

A handout like "First Aid for Electronic Searching" (see Handout 7.2, p. 84) can be kept near all computer stations. Different sections, or even just a rule or two from a section, can be blown up and hung as posters. If several students are having a search crisis at the same time, I can diagnose the nature of each problem and direct individuals to the appropriate section of "First Aid." Then I am free to help the one who is most confused. If the handout proves helpful, a student is likely to remember and use it again.

Too often students walk away from a search muttering that the library has absolutely no information on their topic when even a moment's reflection would convince them that this is unlikely. If "First Aid" is handy, they are more likely to stop and reflect. A heightened awareness of the plethora of rules for computer searching should lead students to the conclusion that computers are extremely rigid, despite all the wonderful things they can do. They are unable to guess what a user is thinking, and so searchers must play by the computer's rules to be successful. Reviewing the rules—and choosing appropriate ones—is a natural extension of the problem-solving process.

Technology Competencies

My exploration of thoughtful researching began many years ago with the realization that a successful search for resources will not, by itself, ensure a well-executed research project. This led me to identify and articulate the other process steps necessary for effective research. I did not abandon the teaching of search skills, but it was certainly not my major focus.

One day, I woke up and realized that technology had made search skills a paramount issue for librarians. Some colleagues seemed to be focusing almost exclusively on teaching students to search with the new high tech tools. I saw how easily my energy and attention might be completely absorbed by technology. It seemed ironic that technology, which had wondrously extended our ability to locate useful information, might end up limiting my ability to teach students to make good use of that information. Was I about to come full circle, back to where I had started, with search skills claiming the lion's share of instructional time?

I received help in sorting out this problem from an unexpected quarter. My district's school board passed a measure calling for technology assessments. The board had spent considerable funds on new technology, but members were uncertain about the impact technology was having on learning. Some buildings and some teachers used technology extensively, although others did not. The board was concerned about equity. They asked each school to identify specific technical competencies that all students would be expected to master at each grade level. A number of areas were designated for assessment, including word processing, multimedia production, data processing, and location of information.

Choose the Most Basic Skills

When I sat down with teachers in my building to choose the information skills for our sixth, seventh, and eighth graders, I realized I had a marvelous opportunity. We were going to pinpoint the most basic skills and make sure all students mastered them. What, we asked ourselves, did we want our students to be able to do? Figuring this out proved fairly simple. Every sixth grader should be able to perform a subject search on the OPAC that would lead to the location of a book on the library shelves. Every seventh grader should be able to use both the subject and keyword search functions of our CD-ROM periodical index to find a relevant article. Every eighth grader should be able to track down information using a search engine on the World Wide Web.

The forms we filled out for the school board required us to describe our standards for student achievement and to indicate how we planned to assess mastery. We were also asked to address the issue of remediation for students who failed to meet the standards. It was breathtaking to consider. I had always wanted all my students to be able to use the catalog effectively, but I had never felt that I achieved this ideal. Now I had a chance to design a program that would make the ideal a reality.

The board would require a report on our level of success. Teachers could not decide at the last minute that it was impossible to fit this instruction into their curricula. We also could not just assume that the instruction had been effective; we had to test it to make sure it was. When the testing uncovered students who had not mastered the skills, we had to do our best to help those students master them.

Design an Assessment Strategy

I needed efficient methods for teaching and assessing. I decided to use volunteers to do performance assessments. These volunteers went through training to learn how to use our OPAC, and then practiced assessing each other using the six criteria for a successful search. We found that five volunteers could easily assess a class of 30 in a single period.

A volunteer would introduce him or herself to a student and then remain silent. He or she simply watched the student perform a search and checked off whether the student met the criteria. When a student ran into difficulty, volunteers offered no prompts. Students who could not complete a search were gently told to return to their classrooms and were informed that they would receive more instruction so that they might be able to pass the test. Amazingly, very few students failed the test the first time, and only a handful never passed it. The few who never passed had serious language problems; they could barely read or were still struggling to become fluent in English.

Our assessment criteria were simple. Students had to select a subject search, not author or title, and use appropriate search words. They had to choose the correct functions to find titles—two steps on our software. Before setting off to find a book, they had to determine whether it was currently available in our library. Some students performed the computer steps brilliantly, but needed a refresher on Dewey decimal numbers to actually locate the physical book.

Select an Instructional Method

I provided small group instruction on how to use the OPAC because I wanted all students to be involved. I asked many questions. Which function key do you think will show you the titles? Which words tell you if the book is in the library right now? Students were asked to use the information on the screen to come up with solutions. The instruction included a few things that were not part of the assessment criteria, like keyword searching, and the use of on-screen information to evaluate the suitability of a book. I also stressed that although the basics of searching would probably remain the same, the software would continue to change and add new features.

In our small groups, everyone had a chance to use the keyboard during instruction. Each student finished up by doing an individual search at a separate terminal. Students who had difficulty were encouraged to come to the library during lunch or before or after school, to practice for their tests.

A few days before the test, the entire class practiced searching through a spirited team "competition." Each team received a card with a different subject on it. They were not given a new card until they presented a relevant book as proof they had completed a search. The team that found the most books "won." As much as possible, we tried to time the instruction and testing to precede an assignment that would require searching on the catalog.

We have added these technology proficiencies one grade at a time. The following year, in seventh grade, I used stations with written instructions to teach students how to do subject and keyword searches on our

CD-ROM magazine index. I roamed about and coached students who had difficulty at the stations. Everyone filled out a worksheet, and this helped me determine who was still confused. For their assessment, students located an article for a science assignment.

My next challenge is to determine exactly how we will teach all eighth graders to use the Web. About half our students need no instruction; many could probably teach *me* a few tricks. The other half do not have computers at home, and many become easily frustrated when they try searching on their own. Those who continue to struggle bravely are often handicapped by gaps in their knowledge of basic operations. One student lamented that she was afraid she would not be able to return to a helpful site. She had no idea that the site's address was right on the screen or that she could bookmark the site. Class discussions of useful addresses had apparently meant nothing to her, because she had no context in which she could fit them.

My current inclination is to use experienced searchers as peer teachers for the students who lack experience. After choosing the basic skills we want all students to master, the next step will be to design a pretest. Students wanting to become peer teachers would have to pass the pretest and go through a training session. The pretest as well as a post-test would again be administered by adult volunteers.

I have not related all this because I think we have found the most basic technology competencies for all middle schools. Our district uses site-based management, so different buildings chose different proficiencies. Not all middle schools felt basic OPAC use was a concern, but, with our population, it definitely was. Other schools were free to focus on more sophisticated types of OPAC searches, or the use of CD-ROM encyclopedias, or whatever seemed to meet their needs.

I believe it is useful to identify a set of search skills for each grade level, and assess for mastery. I would attempt to do this even if I moved to a district that did not require it. When students achieve a basic level of competence with a few types of search software, they are more likely to be comfortable using a problem-solving approach to searching. Of course, students must have opportunities during real assignments to practice their skills, or October's competence may vanish by June.

Some Enduring Skills for Print Resources

The Dewey Decimal System

Proficiency in using the OPAC will amount to little if a student is unable to locate books on the library shelves. Decimals are challenging for many middle school students, especially when they extend several places beyond the decimal point. Many sixth graders will see ".9" as smaller than ".351." A math teacher struggling to convince students that decimals are important in real life may find a library activity the perfect opportunity. Students can apply their math skills as they locate library books. If students do not do well in this practical application, the math teacher will be alerted to the need for reteaching and remediation.

Browsing

Students should understand that each Dewey number is a code for a specific subject. Once they truly comprehend this, they will be open to the suggestion that not every single useful title need be found on an OPAC screen. As long as they find a single relevant title, and a call number, they are ready to become the Sherlock Holmes of the bookshelves, looking at other titles with the same call number to see if they contain useful information.

Finding Information Within Sources

Middle school students usually want a book whose title closely matches their subject. If the topic is festivals of China, they want a book called *Festivals of China*. If reminded, they will agree that a book on festivals will probably include some Chinese ones, and a book on China will probably have a section on festivals. But this is not a natural way for most of them to think. Similarly, most know how to use an index, but they must be constantly reminded of its usefulness in particular situations, or they simply will not think of using it. These two attitudinal stumbling blocks make locating information within sources a neglected skill for most middle school students.

Sometimes teachers want to save the time required for student searching by having the teacher-librarian pull a cart of useful resources instead. A problem—no chance for students to practice search skills—can be turned into an opportunity. A mini-lesson primes students to find information within the already pulled sources. As they look at transparencies of indexes, students locate pages with pertinent information. This can serve as bait to lure them into using the indexes of the books on their resource cart.

The Reference Collection

Most elementary schools have limited reference collections. Sixth-grade orientation is the time to introduce the idea that reference books exist on just about any topic one might want to explore. Present a variety of reference sources that will be useful in upcoming sixth-grade units. Include reference books that have recreational reading appeal, such as encyclopedias about sports or mythology or horses or dogs. It will make the reference section an attractive place to which students will voluntarily return. When they do return, a "Reference Book of the Week" display can encourage them to explore unfamiliar reference sources. Placing print and electronic reference sources in the same area of the library also increases awareness.

Whatever marketing approach you take, most students will still need reminders throughout their middle school years of the wonders of the print reference collection. Nothing beats putting the right source for a specific task in a student's hands at the just the right moment. Handouts geared to specific assignments can also be helpful. Even if many students never bother to read handouts, their teachers do, and they can call useful books to their students' attention.

HOW CAN WE TEACH SEARCH SKILLS?

Small Group, Hands-On Learning

Whenever possible, it is best to teach electronic searching through small group, hands-on lessons. However, there is not enough time in the school year to teach all skills in the manner described for OPAC searching. Sometimes, though, an entire class will not need small group instruction for a particular skill, and the students who do need it can form one group. Perhaps a class contains a cluster of students who have recently moved to the district and who need to catch up on skills other students have already mastered. A group of special needs students may find guided searching in a group far more beneficial than working on their own.

The major virtue of hands-on work is that students can try out the skills and make mistakes. Making mistakes is a productive way to learn; students remember the things they didn't get right the first time. Communicate a "you can do it" attitude while providing plenty of support. Ask questions, and let students solve problems; don't just walk them through a sequence of steps.

Of course, a teacher does not have to be present for students to experience hands-on learning. Providing written instructions seems like an efficient method—if only students would read them. One way to make sure they read the instructions is to include them as part of a station that students will visit during a research unit. The task at a station might be to gather up-to-date information on something like Russia's space program or weapons situation. If the tool for gathering this information is a CD-ROM magazine index, then students will read the instructions to find out how to use it.

Not all hands-on search instruction need involve a computer. Kinesthetic learners may have an easier time with the Dewey Decimal System if they can touch and move the numbers. Strips of tagboard, with call number labels, can stand in for book spines, and students can move them around until they are in perfect shelf order. Students can become the books themselves, holding up cards with call numbers and attempting to put themselves in order. Or they can take turns putting each other in order.

Direct Instruction to Large Groups

Presenting search skills to a full class is something that should be done sparingly. It is not a good way to introduce complex skills. As each new transparency appears on the screen, a few more students will lose interest. Some concrete learners probably tuned out as soon as the lesson began. But not everything can be taught in small groups; there simply isn't time.

Time is a key element in designing an effective large group presentation of search skills. Mini-lessons at the start of a research period work best. Choose a fairly simple skill that builds on ones already mastered. A mini-lesson can also be the most efficient way to introduce new features in familiar software.

Some skills do not require hands-on practice, for instance, identifying keywords, or broadening and narrowing searches. Even here, it is a lot easier to communicate the possibilities and pitfalls of Boolean searching if students are able to see the results of their choices.

Teachable moments often present the best opportunity for mini-lessons. If students seem to be having the same sorts of problems when searching, the time may be ripe for a mini-lesson on possible solutions. Using a real-life situation and examples always heightens interest, since many students will feel a need for this information. Such a lesson may be presented at the end of the period when frustration or confusion motivates students to listen closely, or at the start of a new period when energy and optimism have returned. Occasionally, it may even be worthwhile to call everyone together briefly in the middle of a period.

Coaching

Sometimes, the best way to help a student learn is not through small or large group instruction. One-on-one coaching may be the answer. By the time students have reached sixth grade they often do not want to ask for help (Solomon 1994). When asked how they are doing, they may answer "fine," whether this is true or not. In addition to watching for students who appear to be struggling, a teacher-librarian can also set out with a specific coaching goal. Maybe an assignment will require most students to use the subject keyword function on the OPAC, or perhaps they will need to limit their searches with a "not." Through questioning individual students, the teacher-librarian can increase awareness of these strategies.

Students often lose the opportunity to be coached while searching on the OPAC when a teacher has several sections working on the same project. If the first section finds most of the books, the teacher may request that they be put on a cart for the other groups. It is worth going to the trouble of reshelving the books to avoid this. Even when there is no open period between two classes, the teacher can delay the arrival of the second class by going over assignment instructions in the classroom, or giving a spelling test, or whatever works for him or her. If a teacher is not interested in doing this, make sure a different period goes first each time there is a new research assignment. If first period found most of the books last time, let second period start their research a day earlier when the next assignment begins.

Peer Teaching

Some students, especially those who have a computer at home, may know everything there is to know about using their CD-ROM encyclopedias. Others may have logged countless hours surfing the Web. It pays to make sure a student is as competent as he or she claims to be, but once you have verified proficiency, you can press this expert into service. Occasionally a student may have poor communication skills, but most students enjoy sharing their knowledge and teaching others what they know. Student experts can be given formal assignments. They can also be enlisted on the spot when another student needs help, but the librarian is busy. Just shout out your need. "Who can show Yuri how to bookmark a Web site?"

When you have coached someone through searching with a specific tool, you can ask that student to show the next person. You might want to have the student begin the next research period by telling the class about the search. The peer teacher benefits from this, too. One of the best ways to understand something is to teach it.

Students can also communicate their understanding to others in writing. Writing about a favorite Web search engine, with explanations of why they like it and how to use it, might earn them extra credit in their language arts class.

INSTILLING CONFIDENCE

Listen carefully, and you will notice that adults are always asking questions. A discussion of composting leads someone to wonder how earthworms reproduce. A dinner party conversation about angels leaves a roomful of guests struggling to name all the different kinds—cherubim, seraphim, archangel . . . but watch, and you will see that people rarely bother to pursue the answers, even when they may be close at hand. They do not see the world as a place where they can search for information and find it.

If we want our students to become adults who pursue their curiosity, attitude is fundamental; they must believe they can successfully locate the information they need. Technology ensures that methods for searching will continue to evolve and change. A problem-solving search process makes it possible to confront and make sense of unfamiliar tools. People who do not believe they can locate information will become disabled citizens in our information society. They will also miss out on a lot of fun. The story of earthworm reproduction turns out to be a fascinating one.

REFERENCES

Solomon, Paul. 1994. Children, technology, and instruction: A case study of elementary school children using an on-line public access catalog (OPAC). In "Current research," ed. Delia Neuman. *School Library Media Quarterly* 23 (fall): 48.

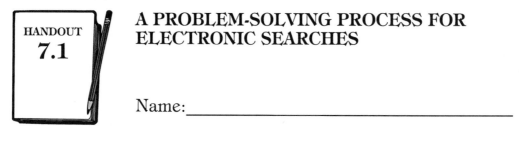

A PROBLEM-SOLVING PROCESS FOR ELECTRONIC SEARCHES

Name:_____

- What are my questions? What do I need to know?

- What search words will help me locate information?

- What are the narrowest, most specific terms, ones that most closely match my questions?

- Circling keywords in my research questions may be helpful.

- Are there synonyms for these search words—words that mean almost the same thing?

- What are some broader terms that may include some information on my topic?

Handout 7.1—*Continued*

- What kind(s) of information do I need?

  _____Brief overview

  _____Short answer to simple question

  _____In-depth information

  _____Data—facts, numbers, statistics

  _____Opinions

- What search tools will I use to locate information?

  _____OPAC—On-line Public Access Catalog

  _____Reference CD-ROMs

  _____Magazine index on CD-ROM

  _____World Wide Web search engines

  _____World Wide Web sites with links to other useful sites

- What types of searches are available on each tool, and which ones will be most useful to me?

  _____Subject

  _____Author

  _____Title

  _____Keyword

  _____Boolean (allows combining search words with terms *and, or,* and *not*)

  _____Full text

  _____Call Number

- How can I find out more about how a search tool works?

  _____Are there "search tips" included in the tool that I can read?

  _____Are there on-screen directions?

  _____Are there pull-down menus that may contain useful options?

  _____Is there a help feature?

  _____Will I need to ask a library staff member for help?

Search not going well? See "FIRST AID FOR ELECTRONIC SEARCHING."

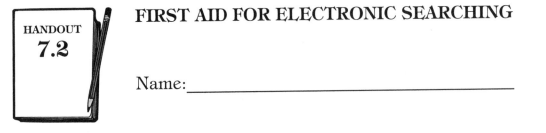

FIRST AID FOR ELECTRONIC SEARCHING

Name:_____

What to Do When You Do Not Find Anything on Your Topic

- Have someone check your spelling.

- Do not use "The" or "A" or "An" when it is the first word in a title.

- Apply the "plurals rule"

    —always use plurals on the OPAC (On-line Public Access Catalog), e.g., tigers not tiger

    —avoid plurals on the Web, e.g., dog, not dogs

- Remember, last names come first on the OPAC, e.g., Lincoln, Abraham, not Abraham Lincoln.

- The OPAC has rules about words that can be used as subjects, for example, automobiles, not cars; agriculture, not farming. Ask a library staff member to help you look up the subject you used in the rule book, *Library of Congress Subject Headings*.

- If searching on the OPAC, try broadening your topic. For example, a book on China may have a section on Buddhism. Then use the book's index and table of contents to locate information.

- Sometimes a title keyword search on the OPAC brings results when nothing else will.

- Using "and" limits results to items containing *all* search words. You may really want "or"—it means an item must have *only one* of the words.

- If searching on the Web, try broadening your search by using * to include all possible endings for a search word, for example, migrat* for migration, migrate, migrates, migratory.

- If searching on the Web, try another search engine. Different engines yield different results.

Handout 7.2—*Continued*

- If you have used only one search tool, try a different one: the OPAC, the Web, reference CD-ROMS, the magazine index on CD-ROM.

- Ask a library staff member to suggest some reference books or alternative search words.

What to Do When You Find Very Little on Your Topic

- If you have found a book on your topic, use its call number to:

  —look for other books with the same number on the nonfiction shelves

  —look for other books with the same number in the reference section

  —do a call number search on the OPAC to locate books in other libraries, then request them through interlibrary loan

- On the OPAC, at the bottom of the "Full Display" screen for a book title, you will find the other subjects for that title. Try searching using these subjects.

- If you have found a site on the Web, check to see if it has links to other sites. Run your mouse over possible linking words; double click when a little hand appears over a word.

- Look for links in CD-ROM articles, too.

- Review the suggestions for "What to Do When You Do Not Find Anything on Your Topic."

What to Do When You Find Too Much on Your Topic

This is for those times when the screen says "752 results."

- Try narrowing your search using "and" to add search words that more precisely define what you are looking for, for example, not just hockey, but hockey AND rules.

- Limit your search with "not," for example, dolphin NOT football.

- If you used a keyword search on the magazine index CD-ROM, try a subject search.

REMEMBER, it is a sign of intelligence to ask for help when you need it.

From *The Thoughtful Researcher.* © 1999 Libraries Unlimited. (800) 237-6124.

CHAPTER 8

Evaluating Sources

Thinking Critically

Four students, burdened with stacks of books, staggered into the library a few minutes before the end of the period. They were the very same group that had arrived in a state of high excitement at the beginning of the period. They had used the OPAC to locate resources for their Asian studies project. They had been pleased with the results. They had checked out many books, apparently the very same books they were now dropping in the book return.

"You've finished with all of them already?" asked the astonished teacher-librarian.

Annie explained that she was returning six of her seven books because they had absolutely nothing to do with her topic, the Cultural Revolution. The librarian noticed that several of her books were about ancient China, and another focused solely on Chinese geography. Lim was in the same predicament as Annie. He had found several books recounting Chinese history, but they all stopped well before the events in Tiananmen Square in 1989. He now realized that the books had been published before those events ever happened.

Selina also insisted that her books had no information on her topic, education in Japan. Looking down at the three shiny series books in Selina's hands, the librarian wondered if this could possibly be true, and asked if she could check. The indexes showed that all the books had extensive information on education.

"Oh," murmured Selina, "I forgot about the index."

Jason had found only one very fat volume, and he parted with it now. It was certainly about the Vietnam War, but he had not been able to understand anything in its 550 pages.

JUDGING THE USEFULNESS OF SOURCES— THREE BASIC QUESTIONS

Far too many middle school students use a single standard for assessing the success of an information search, and that standard is quantitative. They found five books or two Web sites or one extremely long article in an electronic encyclopedia. They believe these sources have something to do with their topics, but more often than not, they have not bothered to check. The result is likely to be the disappointment faced by the four Asian studies students, who would not have wasted a full period had they remembered a few simple criteria for evaluating their sources before checking them out.

Does This Resource Relate to My Topic and Questions?

If Annie had used the indexes in her books, she would have known right away that most were not useful, and she could have continued her search or asked for help. If Selina had remembered the index, she would have located information on her topic; she could then have spent her time reading instead of hopelessly thumbing through her books. Skimming (see Chapter 10) would have proved useful, once the index directed her to the relevant pages. Skimming would also have helped other class members who neglected to give even a glance to the screens of their electronic sources before printing.

Is My Information Up-to-Date?

Using the index would also have told Lim that none of his books talked about Tiananmen Square. He might have determined this even more easily if he had checked the books' copyright dates, something he could have done right on the OPAC. Of course, he would have needed to know when the events in Tiananmen happened. Unfortunately, no presearch had preceded his search, so he did not.

In many cases, students will not need the information gleaned in a presearch to decide whether they need current information. If they want to learn about space stations or computers, a ten-year-old book simply won't do. On the other hand, if they are inquiring about a Civil War battle or the habits of honey bees, the copyright date will not be an issue.

Can I Read This Information?

Many middle schools serve diverse populations, and the range of reading levels in the library collection is one reflection of this diversity. Gifted students may need challenging materials that would be appropriate in a high school collection. Students who are just becoming literate in English will have more success if they can find information written for elementary readers. When the collection contains resources for students reading above, below, and at grade level, determining the readability of resources becomes a crucial skill.

Fortunately, the "five finger rule" works well and almost any student can understand and apply it. The reader simply opens to a random page in a book and begins to read. A finger goes up for each word he or she cannot understand. Five fingers up before the end of the page means the source is likely to be too difficult. Since most of the information on the Internet is aimed at adult readers, students should use the five finger rule when looking at Web sites.

OPPORTUNITIES FOR JUDGING THE USEFULNESS OF SOURCES

Start with the OPAC

The criteria for judging the usefulness of sources can easily become part of basic instruction in use of the OPAC. After demonstrating a subject search, I ask students to scan the list of titles on the screen for helpful information about each book. The titles themselves may offer clues about a book's contents, and the copyright dates indicate whether a book is up-to-date.

The display for an individual title provides additional clues for forming a judgment. The number of pages in a book can be very important to a middle school reader. A lengthy book is often challenging. In addition, a slow reader may decide he or she will not have enough time to read several hundred pages. Bright students sometimes think length is an indication of quality, so it is worth pointing out that the book may still prove useless if none of the pages relates to a student's research questions.

Most sixth graders, even if they used the OPAC frequently in elementary school, have never noticed that the title screen contains a summary of a book's contents. Even when the summary seems to indicate that a book contains relevant information, I remind students to check the book's index to make sure.

I plant the idea, early in sixth grade, that there is more to a successful information search than simply finding a resource.

Use Encyclopedias to Practice Evaluating Sources

I water the seed of evaluation skills through an activity that allows students to practice applying them. This, too, is best done early in sixth grade. Encyclopedias make great source material for an activity. Students have used them frequently in elementary school and feel comfortable with them. Now they will see encyclopedias in a new light as they compare them to specific criteria. Aha, they realize, research in middle school is going to be different.

Because encyclopedia articles tend to be brief, an activity that involves comparing two articles can be completed in a single class period. What students learn from the comparison may be the whole point of the exercise, or they may also need to come away with some specific information about a topic. Keeping the information need simple and containing the activity to a single day makes it easier to fit such an activity into an already crowded curriculum. A comparison of encyclopedia articles can also be done at the beginning of a research project when students must start with basic overview material.

The criteria for evaluating encyclopedia articles contain the three basic questions for judging sources, but go beyond them (see Handout 8.1, p. 98). The additional criteria were identified through a task analysis (see Chapter 2). As I reviewed a number of encyclopedia articles, I watched for factors that seemed important. I realized that length was an issue; sometimes I wanted the quickest answer; sometimes I required details. Cross-references occasionally helped me track down details, so they seemed an important feature. I was surprised to discover that some articles treated a subject from several angles, for example, scientific, historical, and geographical, so I added "variety." Some treatments were dry as dust; I wanted interesting material. I was disappointed whenever there was no accompanying visual material, but I also discovered that some visuals added nothing to my understanding.

A comparison of two encyclopedias will not always lead to a clear-cut winner. Sometimes the verdict will be mixed; one may offer the most readable text, while another may contain outstanding pictorial information. Choosing the best one is not the point of the exercise. Students may learn that although one resource answers some needs, another proves useful for completely different reasons.

Require Evaluation of Sources for Independent Projects

A process step requiring students to evaluate their resources, using the three basic criteria, is tailor-made for independent projects where students have chosen their own topics. Once students stray off the curricular map with subjects like "the history of wine making," the library collection, and indeed the Internet and the public library, may not always meet their information needs. If students evaluate their sources early, they will avoid a crisis later. If they do not find enough information, they should be allowed to change topics. If they conclude that they have enough information, they cannot use lack of information as an excuse later. Handout 8.2 (p. 99), provides students with strategies for answering the three questions.

USING CRITICAL THINKING SKILLS TO EVALUATE THE QUALITY OF INFORMATION

The new information literacy standards of the American Association of School Librarians and the Association for Educational Communications and Technology (AASL and AECT 1998) include the ability to evaluate information critically. Once students have found sources that appear useful, critical thinking skills (Beyer 1987) can help students assess the quality of the information a source contains (see Fig. 8.1).

Mastery of these thinking skills requires considerable practice over time. Students will need to work with short pieces of writing on a variety of topics. Trying to introduce the skills in the library as part of a research unit can be difficult; the classroom environment provides more opportunities for practice. Still, as teacher-librarian, you have an important role to play; you can work to ensure that the skills are actually taught.

Fig. 8.1. Critical Thinking Skills

1. Distinguishing between verifiable facts and value claims

2. Distinguishing relevant from irrelevant information, claims, or reasons

3. Determining the factual accuracy of a statement

4. Determining the credibility of a source

5. Identifying ambiguous claims or arguments

6. Identifying unstated assumptions

7. Detecting bias

8. Identifying logical fallacies

9. Recognizing logical inconsistencies in a line of reasoning

10. Determining the strength of an argument or claim

From Beyer, Barry K. *Practical strategies for the teaching of thinking.*
© 1987 by Allyn & Bacon. Reprinted by permission.

If critical thinking skills are not part of your school's curriculum, you will have to convince someone that they should be. How you go about this will probably depend on the situation in your particular building. Look for opportunities. If your school is implementing a "reading across the curriculum" program, people who have never taught reading may welcome concrete suggestions on how to carry out new responsibilities. Or you may want to begin with a small group—an interdisciplinary team, a particular grade level, one department, or some of the usual risk takers.

Models for the Teaching of Critical Thinking Skills

You will want to present teachers with models for teaching the skills. However, I have not always found it easy to determine exactly how specific critical thinking skills should be taught. These skills, so crucial in evaluating information, are often merely mentioned and sometimes overlooked altogether in the professional literature, regardless of whether an author is focusing on a thinking skills curriculum, or on the research process itself. The teaching of critical thinking is an area I have only recently started to explore, so I can only offer a few early models.

An easier task is to support classroom instruction by finding reading materials to use with a particular skill. Newspapers and magazines are full of writing that displays a particular point of view or bias. Out-of-date books that must be weeded from the collection provide a gold mine of information to be checked for accuracy. A cross section of pre-selected sites on the Internet supply the raw material for determining the relevancy of information as well as the credibility of a source. Literature, particularly picture books and short stories, offers a good place to start applying many of these skills.

No matter what the skill being taught, it is best to begin with a definition of that skill and then determine what students may already know about the skill as defined. This instructional technique is outlined in the lesson on summarizing (see Chapter 9). When you have compared students' prior knowledge of the skill to the recommended strategy, the whole class should practice applying the skill with the teacher. Next comes independent practice, with students working in pairs; because these are complex skills, discussion helps. Conclude with an examination of problems, insights, and new discoveries. This approach is adapted from the work of Beyer (1985), who has written extensively on the teaching of thinking skills.

Identifying Point of View

Students often have an accepting attitude toward anything that appears in print. If it is there in black and white, it must be true. It rarely occurs to them that books and articles and Web pages may contain opinions as well as facts. Sometimes a particularly extreme statement serves to remind them that not everything they read is "true." While determining point of view does not appear on the list of ten critical thinking skills, I consider it a helpful preliminary skill if students are to be able to detect bias and distinguish facts from value claims.

Literature offers a great starting point for the consideration of point of view. Many stories are told from the point of view of several characters. The whole genre of "fractured" fairy tales is built on a change in the point of view. When students recognize what a difference point of view makes in our understanding of a story, they can move on to nonfiction writing. It is important to teach for transfer by reviewing the steps for identifying point of view and calling attention to their usefulness in evaluating nonfiction.

I used a task analysis (see Chapter 2) to develop the lesson on point of view (see Fig. 8.2).

Fig. 8.2. Identifying Point of View

DEFINITION

Point of view is the position from which a person observes or considers something. Many factors shape our point of view—age, personality, family background, culture, beliefs, experiences.

STEPS TO USE WHEN IDENTIFYING POINT OF VIEW

1. Determine the main topic, the subject of your reading.

2. Identify the parts of the subject to which the author gives most attention. What is repeated? Emphasized? What is his or her concern?

3. Identify aspects of the subject the author ignores or mentions only briefly.

4. Locate words or phrases that suggest how the author <u>feels</u> about the subject.

5. Note any unstated assumptions, things the author seems to take for granted.

6. Based on the evidence gathered by following steps 1–5, summarize the author's point of view.

Distinguishing Between Facts and Value Claims

Many middle school students find ethical questions and moral arguments fascinating. They are likely to be sympathetic to strongly held and strongly stated opinions. Learning to distinguish facts from value claims gives them the ability to distance themselves from the feeling tone of a piece of writing and thoughtfully consider its content. The ability to distinguish facts from value claims helps students recognize bias.

The strategy for distinguishing facts from value claims (see Fig. 8.3, p. 94) is adapted from material from the Tahoma School District (Skerritt 1997), and the work of Stripling and Pitts (1988, 113).

Fig. 8.3. Distinguishing Between Facts, Opinions, or Value Claims

DEFINITIONS

Facts are provable statements.

Opinions or value claims represent an author's belief or judgment.

STEPS TO USE WHEN DISTINGUISHING FACTS FROM OPINIONS OR VALUE CLAIMS

1. Review the reading.

2. Identify provable facts using these clues:
   - Footnoted information
   - Active verbs, or present and past tenses of the verb "to be": is, was, has been
   - Statistics
   - Specific details that you can check

3. Identify opinions using the following clues:
   - Statements reflecting personal beliefs—"I think," "I believe," "In my opinion"
   - Subjunctive verbs—could, might, would
   - Qualifying statements with terms like "probably," "maybe"
   - Judgmental terms to indicate something is good or bad
   - Hypothetical situations—"If . . . "
   - Predictions of future events

4. Identify value claims by looking for words that place a statement in a range from good to bad—"finest," "worst," "outrageous."

5. Compare the number of factual statements to the number of opinions or values.

Recognizing Bias

In an age when sound bites and inflamed rhetoric often carry the day, students must learn to recognize bias. We must teach them to consider whether a journalist has presented more than one side in coverage of an issue, for there is always more than one side, and sometimes several sides. Students should consider different sides of an issue before drawing conclusions, and then present arguments supporting their conclusions.

When teaching students to recognize bias, use material on topics about which students are unlikely to have strong opinions. If they have already formed a deeply held belief about a "hot" issue, such as abortion or gun control, they will not be able to calmly and rationally apply the strategy for recognizing bias.

The steps for recognizing bias (see Fig. 8.4) are adapted from the thinking skills curriculum of the Tahoma School District (Skerritt 1997).

Fig. 8.4. Recognizing Bias

DEFINITION

Bias is a one-sided point of view.

STEPS TO USE WHEN RECOGNIZING BIAS

1. Determine the main topic, the subject of your reading.

2. Identify possible points of view on this topic.

3. Review the writing for these bias clues:

    • Over-generalizations—"Everyone knows . . . " "Nobody would ever . . . " "All sensible people . . . "

    • Appeals to the reader's feelings or emotions

    • Exaggeration

    • Stereotypes

    • Opinions stated as facts

    • Imbalance in presentation—Is the "other side" thoughtfully considered?

4. Based on the evidence from the clues, decide if the author is biased.

5. If yes, state the author's bias.

If you wish to teach one of the other critical thinking skills but are unsure exactly what to do, try a task analysis (see Chapter 2). Consider the steps you go through as you attempt to apply the skill. If you are interested in developing lessons for the critical thinking skills relating to logic, Stripling and Pitts (1988, 114–15) provide some useful material to jump-start your thinking. If someone in your building teaches logic, that person may be willing to collaborate with you.

Integrate Critical Thinking into Research Assignments

Once students have had some practice in applying critical thinking skills, it's time to start integrating them into appropriate library research assignments. If students are exploring controversial issues, require an annotated bibliography that evaluates every source for bias. It does not really matter if a source turns out to be biased or balanced; students will have practice in making that judgment. During Internet research, provide a simple log where students record the name of each site visited and a brief assessment of its relevancy and credibility. When students keep journals during their research, they can record instances of checking for factual accuracy, distinguishing facts from value claims, or employing any other critical thinking skills you may wish to highlight.

I have just suggested a logical progression that begins with persuading colleagues to teach these skills and ends with designing assignments that require students to apply them. However, you may have to take the back door to thinking skills instruction and begin with a proposed assignment. If an assignment will require use of the Internet, suggest some practice first in determining relevancy and credibility of sources. If a teacher is planning a unit on controversial issues, offer materials that teach students to recognize bias and to distinguish facts from value claims.

THOUGHTFUL SELECTION OF SOURCES— A MATTER OF READINESS

Critical thinking skills are sophisticated thought processes that may prove difficult for younger middle school students who have not yet begun to think abstractly. Eighth or ninth grade may prove the most effective time to teach students strategies for evaluating the quality of the information found in a source. The three basic questions for judging the usefulness of a source can be understood and asked by any middle school student. Once we have made students aware of this crucial step in the research process, we must train them to perform it routinely. A thoughtful researcher should take the time to judge the usefulness of any source he or she locates.

REFERENCES

American Association of School Librarians (AASL) and Association for Educational Communications and Technology (AECT). 1998. *Information Literacy Standards for Student Learning.* Chicago: American Library Association. 8.

Beyer, Barry K. 1985. Practical strategies for the direct teaching of thinking skills in *Developing minds: A resource book for teaching thinking*, ed. Arthur L. Costa. Arlington, VA: Association for Supervision and Curriculum Development. 145–50.

———. 1987. *Practical strategies for the teaching of thinking.* Boston: Allyn & Bacon. 44.

Skerritt, Nancy. 1997. *Literature study guide: Using thinking skills and graphic organizers with literature.* Maple Valley, WA: Tahoma School District. Unpaged.

Stripling, Barbara K., and Judy M. Pitts. 1988. *Brainstorms and blueprints: Teaching library research as a thinking process.* Englewood, CO: Libraries Unlimited.

| HANDOUT 8.1 | CRITERIA FOR EVALUATING ENCYCLOPEDIA ARTICLES |

Name:_____

Topic:_____

Encyclopedia:_____

1. Relevance—Does the information help me to answer my questions about the topic?

2. Copyright date—Is this information up-to-date? Do I need recent information?

3. Readability—Can I understand the information?

4. Length—Do I find enough information for my purpose? Too little?

5. Variety—Do I find information on different aspects of the topic, for example, scientific, social, historical, geographical?

6. Interest—Is my curiosity about the subject aroused as I read?

7. Pictorial information—Are there illustrations, charts, maps, etc.? Is my understanding increased by them?

8. Cross references—Am I told about other places, within the encyclopedia or outside it, where I can find additional information?

HANDOUT 8.2

JUDGING THE USEFULNESS OF BOOKS AND WEB SITES

Name:_____

Does This Resource Relate to My Topic and Questions?

When using the OPAC:

- Look at the title of a book for clues about its contents.
- Read the "Summary" on the "Full Display" screen for more clues about a book's contents.

When looking at a book:

- Use the index to look up your topic and related keywords.
- Skim the pages listed in the index for information related to your questions.

When searching on the WEB:

- Read the title and description of each item on your results list to find the most helpful ones.

Is My Information Up-to-Date?

When using the OPAC:

- Look at the copyright date for each title. Copyright dates appear on several screens.

When looking at a book:

- Look at the copyright page—it is almost always behind the title page.

Fig. 9.1. Summarizing Strategies

- Find the "keywords" to keep the meaning
- Don't use unnecessary words, especially a, an, the
- Use math symbols: = + -
- Use numbers—2 instead of two
- Try to replace a group of words with one word that means the same thing
- Use "caveman language," never full sentences
- Make lists
- Bullets really help

Now that students know what they are supposed to do, and how they can do it, we practice summarizing three sentences together. It is best to begin with the smallest unit possible, in this case the sentence. Students identify all the words they can eliminate without sacrificing the meaning of the sentence. I cross them out on a transparency. Usually we reach a point where they will have to discuss whether a word is necessary to the meaning of the sentence. Sometimes this depends on the amount of background knowledge the notetaker has. Those who already know that people *throw* a discus and that it's an *event* at the Olympics may not need those words in their notes for it to make sense. Those who have never heard of a discus before may find those words absolutely crucial.

When the class is sure we have only the words we need, the "key" words, each student writes a summarized note. They use the techniques on our list to make their notes as concise as possible. I write their summaries on the overhead. Sometimes there is a class consensus on what makes the best note, but often we have several possibilities, all good—a bulleted list, short phrases, a mathematical style equation. It is very important that they understand there is no single right way to take a note.

After we have practiced together, the class concludes with students working individually to summarize four more sentences. If there is time, and this will depend on the composition of the particular class, we go through the same process of putting the "best" notes on a transparency. If there is no time, I return the next day to debrief at the beginning of class. In any case, I take all their work home to assess how well each student is doing.

A single class on summarizing is not enough for most students to achieve anything near mastery. But practice takes time, and time is a precious commodity in most classrooms. It took me a while to find a teacher willing to give students time to practice summarizing. The results were amazing. She started each class by debriefing three sentences from the previous day. Students who had found elegant ways to use the fewest possible words were eager to share them. Then everyone would practice individually summarizing three new sentences, with many striving to apply the models their classmates had just presented. They improved fast. After a dozen ten-minute practice sessions, they were undoubtedly the best summarizers in the school, and they were sixth graders. They were a heterogeneous group—some very bright, some with special needs, a few seriously at-risk.

The teacher took on the daily chore of looking over their summaries. I knew she might falter if she had to come up with her own sentences every day, so I provided them. Using magazine and encyclopedia articles aimed at this age group, I located sentences that had substantial content, but were stylistically straightforward. Each sentence had to stand on its own and not depend on a preceding or following sentence to make sense. There can still be problems, even when a sentence meets these criteria. One student, trying to decide if she had a keyword, raised her hand to ask what would make a court "supreme." Everyone turned to hear the answer. None of the students knew what the Supreme Court was; many had never even heard of it.

You will find some of the sentences I use with sixth graders in the Appendix. They may save you some of the effort involved in coming up with your own, but they may be too easy or too difficult for the students with whom you will be working. Even when you think you have a list of acceptable sentences, you and your collaborating partner will need to keep your ears open for confusion resulting from a lack of basic knowledge. You may be surprised by what your students do not know.

Finding the Main Idea

Once students know how to summarize, I introduce the skill of finding the main idea. I follow the same instructional format. We come up with a definition of the task, and then list the strategies for accomplishing it (see Fig. 9.2). Sticking to the rule of beginning practice with the smallest unit, we begin with paragraphs. Again, I try the process with the whole class, discussing and critiquing what we are doing as we go; then students work individually.

Fig. 9.2. Main Idea Strategies

- To locate main idea, ask: "What is this paragraph about? What would be its title?"
- Use short phrases to summarize
- Check to make sure all supporting details are included
- Reread to see if note makes sense to you

I often use a web as a graphic organizer for teaching finding the main idea (see Fig. 9.3, p. 104). Students write the main idea in the center circle. They write supporting details in the surrounding circles. This forces them to look for supporting details and to eliminate anything that does not support the main idea. Otherwise, they may end up taking a note that merely applies their summarizing skills to everything in the paragraph. They will have abbreviated the information, but they will not have made sense of it. When they are able to identify main ideas and supporting details consistently, they can start taking ordinary notes, although a few students will prefer to continue using a web.

Fig. 9.3. Main Idea Web

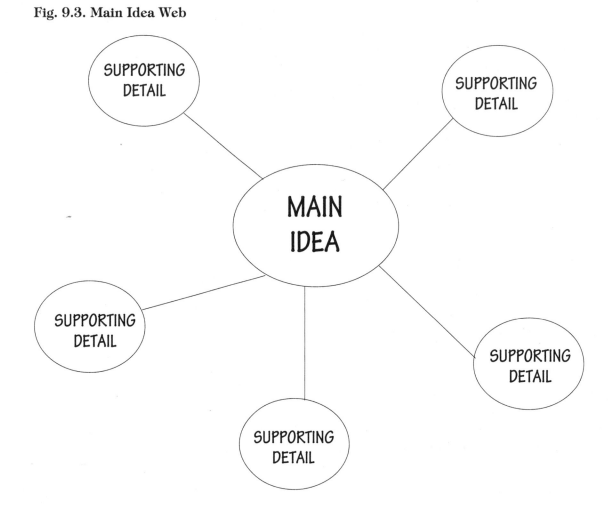

Other Useful Skills

Summarizing and finding the main idea are the most essential prerequisites for taking good notes, and with practice most sixth graders can master them. Paraphrasing, or putting someone else's ideas in your own words, is a lot harder and is usually best taught in eighth grade. Even then, most students will complain that the way the idea was originally expressed sounds best. Admit that it is a challenge and try to make a game of it. Can you come up with a simple yet interesting way to express the same idea? This is a good time to explain that when they do copy another person's words exactly, they must use quotation marks to indicate they have done this.

The ability to classify, or to group things by common characteristics and then assign the groups labels (see Chapter 11), can prevent students from seeing every bit of new information as a main idea. Instead of recording the height, weight, and length of an animal on separate note cards, they will record these facts under the heading size. Classifying is useful both for the actual taking of notes and for organizing the information contained in those notes. Most disciplines use some system of classification. Ask subject-matter teachers how and when they teach classification, so that you can teach for transfer.

A PRESEARCH—THE FOUNDATION FOR GOOD NOTETAKING

Students may have mastered all the prerequisite skills yet still not be able to take good notes when they begin their actual assignments. If they do not know what they are looking for, each piece of information will seem equally important. What should they record? Whatever they find first, until they have recorded "enough" information? Random bits from several sources if three or four are required? Just one encyclopedia article that appears to cover "everything" about a topic?

It is bad enough to have unfocused research questions. Students will be even more confused if they do not possess enough basic information about a topic to understand what they are reading. Lack of comprehension is one of the root causes of plagiarism. A presearch will be essential to provide the background knowledge needed for comprehension of more complex sources. Students can recall their prior knowledge of a topic and explore some overview material when the topic is unfamiliar. Then they will be able to generate questions to guide their research. They will know what kind of information they need and will want the answers. They will also be much more likely to struggle with difficult material to understand the information and make sensible choices about what main ideas to record.

TEACHING A COMPLETE NOTETAKING PROCESS

I reinforce the use of focused research questions by teaching, reteaching, and reinforcing (through posters and handouts) a seven-step notetaking process (see Fig. 9.4, p. 106).

Direct Instruction

I introduce the process after students have developed their own research questions. We practice using an encyclopedia article of seven or eight paragraphs. An enlargement fits nicely on a single transparency and one-page handout, and most slow readers can manage to read it.

I break the seven steps of the process into four transparencies. I begin with the first step at the top of an otherwise blank transparency. Since I teach the process right after students have generated questions for an actual research project, I tell the class they have just completed the first step. By identifying the questions they are going to pursue, they now know what information they are looking for. For practice with the short article, I announce that I will decide what we need to know. I write a question on the transparency, for instance, "What are the treatments of angina pectoris?"

The second transparency contains the second step in the notetaking process plus the article. We go over the strategies for previewing the reading and choose "looking at topic sentences" as the appropriate one for our short article. Students then preview the information by looking at a handout that also contains the article. They find the paragraphs that relate to our question. When they can identify these paragraphs, I mark them on the transparency.

Fig. 9.4. The Notetaking Process

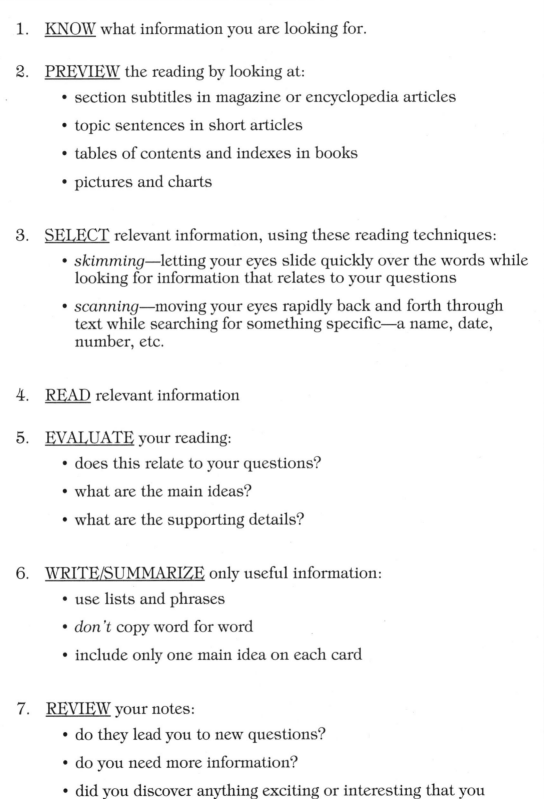

1. <u>KNOW</u> what information you are looking for.

2. <u>PREVIEW</u> the reading by looking at:
    - section subtitles in magazine or encyclopedia articles
    - topic sentences in short articles
    - tables of contents and indexes in books
    - pictures and charts

3. <u>SELECT</u> relevant information, using these reading techniques:
    - *skimming*—letting your eyes slide quickly over the words while looking for information that relates to your questions
    - *scanning*—moving your eyes rapidly back and forth through text while searching for something specific—a name, date, number, etc.

4. <u>READ</u> relevant information

5. <u>EVALUATE</u> your reading:
    - does this relate to your questions?
    - what are the main ideas?
    - what are the supporting details?

6. <u>WRITE/SUMMARIZE</u> only useful information:
    - use lists and phrases
    - *don't* copy word for word
    - include only one main idea on each card

7. <u>REVIEW</u> your notes:
    - do they lead you to new questions?
    - do you need more information?
    - did you discover anything exciting or interesting that you would like to know more about?

Steps 3–6 appear on the same transparency. Step 3, selecting relevant information, really does not apply to such a short piece since they selected the paragraphs they were going to read when they previewed the article. We discuss times when skimming and scanning of longer material will be necessary. They might already have notes on a number of angina treatments and need to find out if they are missing any others. They might be almost finished with their notetaking and looking for very specific information in areas where their research seems incomplete. Or they might just want to make sure that a chapter is relevant.

When we reach Step 4, reading, we reflect that many students would ordinarily start their notetaking here. Now I direct them to read the paragraphs they selected earlier, but warn them that they still may not write. We do not move on to Step 5, evaluating the reading, until everyone has finished the reading. When all agree that the paragraphs do indeed relate to the question, we review the concept of main ideas and supporting details.

It is important to present some concrete examples of main ideas *with* supporting details. I do not ask students to find the main ideas in the article we are using yet; they will do that in a minute when they write their own notes. When students are new to the notetaking process, I usually give an example every day of a main idea with its supporting details. I warn them about the possibility of information being untrue or incorrect if a detail is overlooked. A powerful example comes from a note about using condoms to prevent herpes. It fails to mention that this will only work if no symptoms of the disease are present. We also talk about the plight of students who summarize too much and leave out details, only to find out later that they do not have enough information to understand their notes. These examples come from real students, and recurrent problems with main idea and supporting details have convinced me that it is an area requiring considerable coaching.

When I finally reveal the word *write* on the screen, students can barely restrain themselves. First we review what they know about summarizing. Then, as they write, I am in constant motion. Someone finishes quickly. Okay, I tell her, you have the main ideas, but I do not see any details. Someone is copying. I ask him to see if he can eliminate any of the words he has written and still keep the meaning. If he cannot, I model with one sentence and ask him to try the next. Someone has taken an excellent note but missed a fundamental fact. Go back and see what you have left out, I suggest.

As I circulate, I also look for good examples of different formats. This student has produced a pretty standard outline; that one a simple list with bullets. One person has used short phrases, another a web. I distribute some blank transparencies and pens and ask a few students to copy their notes. I want to show the class that there is no single right way to take a note. I will not embarrass anyone by putting up a bad note, but not every note will be perfect. Since we are engaged in the process of learning how to take better notes, they can all improve as they practice. So we critique the notes as students share them on the overhead: Mike could have eliminated a few unimportant words; Shantae missed one key detail.

Next we answer the questions in Step 7. The two paragraphs on the handout have the high points of angina treatments, but there are always follow-up questions. What is the survival rate for by-pass surgery? How do the different types of pills work? The article mentions nitroglycerin, and someone always wants to know why something used in explosives can also help the human heart. A teacher can tell whether a student is summarizing, or identifying main ideas, or recording relevant information by looking at that student's notes. Step 7 is tougher to assess. I have to be an active coach, prodding and asking questions, to make sure students practice the reflection called for in Step 7.

Coaching

I speak directly about my coaching role before students begin their own notetaking. What would you think of a coach who gave you a lecture on how to hit a baseball, had you try it once, and then wished you good luck? As they shake their heads, I ask what else they would need. When they say they want someone to watch them practice, give them pointers, and answer their questions, I announce that those are exactly the things I will be doing as they take notes. I will be their coach.

Soon after they start taking notes, students begin to ask for help. "I'm not sure if this is a main idea." "I'm having trouble summarizing this." "I can't understand this; what should I do?" Almost always, on the first day, someone will ask, "Do I have to take notes on this page even if it has nothing to do with anything I'm researching?" She already knows the answer, but it is so contrary to anything she has done in the past that she wants reassurance. Later on someone will declare, "This is so much easier," adding sheepishly, "I used to copy *everything.*"

NOTETAKING
PRACTICE DRILLS

If students are about to start a research assignment and have not taken any notes for a while, it is a good idea to have them practice notetaking. After a brief review of what makes a good note, have students take notes by using a common resource. You will want to use their work to assess their readiness, but do not treat the exercise as though it were a test. Move among the students and offer coaching advice. If many are having trouble with a particular skill, you will probably want to reteach it and offer some time to practice. We know that skills become rusty if not used; it may not take much work to bring students back to where they were last semester or before summer vacation. However, in today's mobile society you may also be working with students who did not attend your school when prerequisite skills were taught.

Students generally hate repeating an activity. "We've already done this," they wail. I am including a number of different ways to organize a drill. One may be a better match for a particular assignment or a particular class. Sometimes I will be in charge of the drill with the classroom teacher as assistant coach. If my schedule is crowded, I model the activity during one period and let the teacher use it with her other classes. Another teacher may simply need to read over the possibilities for drills and choose one to use by himself. Some will have their own ways to help students practice notetaking.

No Copying Drill

1. All students read a short encyclopedia article that has a blank cover sheet attached.

2. After reading, students pull the cover sheet over the article, and write the main points that they can remember.

3. Students may reread, looking for supporting details to flesh out their notes.

Main Ideas Drill

1. All students read the same encyclopedia or magazine article.

2. They list 5–10 important words from the text.

3. They write a brief summary note for each word chosen.

4. Classroom teacher or teacher-librarian responds to each student's notes individually.

This drill is based on one developed by Stripling and Pitts (1988, 117)

Categorizing Drill

1. All students read the same short encyclopedia article.

2. They then choose important categories of information contained in the article.

3. Everyone rereads for information, one category at a time.

4. Students take notes on the categories using short phrases.

5. They evaluate their notes:
   • do notes fit categories?
   • do notes make sense?
   • do notes cover all the important facts?
   • are notes in short phrases?

This categorizing drill was inspired by a lesson developed by Sue Black, Bennett Elementary School, Bellevue, WA.

Notes to Prose Drill

1. All students read the same short encyclopedia article.

2. Students write down five brief notes in their own words using sentence fragments.

3. Teacher puts notes on board or overhead, collecting one per student, until there is nothing left to discover.

4. All students use these notes to write individually about the information they have read. Collect the articles first. Encourage creativity in writing.

5. Some students read their writing, demonstrating that the same information can lead to very different final products.

NOTETAKING FORMATS THAT HIGHLIGHT THE RESEARCH QUESTIONS

Students will usually insist that they want to take notes on sheets of paper. It is essential you choose a notetaking format that supports the focus on research questions. If students continue to use paper, and no structure is provided, they will find it hard to break the bad habits they have developed. They will lose sight of their questions and discover too late that they have lots of "background," or "miscellaneous facts."

A Folder for Note Cards

Ignore their cries of protest as you insist they will use note cards. Ignore the voice in the back of your head reminding you that you always hated them too. Explain that you have chosen cards because they will reinforce several things you are determined to reinforce, such as taking notes in the fewest possible words and keeping main ideas separate. A folder with envelopes glued inside will help them select information that relates to their questions. On one of the envelopes they will write *bibliography*, and in it they will keep all their bibliography cards. They will write one of their research questions on each of the other envelopes—three in a letter size folder and five in a legal. Notes relating only to the question on the envelope may be placed inside. A sheet with the assessment criteria for the notes is stapled on the front of the folder (see Fig. 9.5, p. 113). Students will often use it as a checklist to make sure they are doing all the things they need to do. Producing the folders is labor intensive. You will need a cadre of student aides or parent volunteers to glue and staple.

The notes folder is the most frequently used format in my school. For major projects, where students will be gathering a significant amount of information over an extended period of time, it has proved the easiest way to keep students' notes organized.

Notetaking Forms

When students are working on short assignments that take only a day or two, I often use simple forms designed by my colleague in the Bellevue, WA, public schools, Sandy Koehn. The forms, divided in half or into quarters, help students record only information they actually need (see Handout 9.1, p. 116). In a bubble at the top of each section they write a question; for example, How do lions hunt? The small space below reinforces summarizing. These sheets are a good starting place for sixth graders. Yes, you could just have them take their own paper and fold it in half or in quarters. But middle school students respect forms; there is something about those printed black lines that reinforces staying within them.

I have trays with a variety of handouts that students can pick up at any time, and the notetaking forms are always available. If a teacher does not require a particular format for notes, some students will choose to use the forms. Many times, when an assignment has caught me by surprise, I have been grateful for a stack of the notetaking forms ready and waiting. If the teacher has provided the questions for an assignment, students just need to write them in the bubbles. If they have only their topics, we brainstorm possible questions.

One word of caution, though: these forms by themselves will not necessarily lead to quality notes. Students need instruction and coaching in how to use them.

Notes on Gummed Sheets

Here's another "beginner" format that works wonderfully when students are researching in groups. You will need some long strips of butcher paper in different colors. At the top of each strip write a group topic. Then use a yardstick to divide the paper into sections equaling the number of research questions they will pursue. This is a great job for a student aide. If the teacher has assigned research questions, the aide can write them at the top of each section. If students are to generate their own questions, they can write them in later. This works best if you have wall space to hang the butcher paper, but you can also spread the strips out on tables.

You also need some message sheets that have a sticky strip across the top. Give each student a pad of sticky sheets. Ten sheets is a good number to start; they can have more if they use them all. Make these small pads by dividing a large package and using a regular note card as a backing for the bottom sheet. Many of my students have never used these sheets and they are thrilled to have some of their very own. They are note card size, but nobody has ever protested that they are too small for taking notes.

Now comes the fun part. After students complete a note, they stick it on the correct section of their butcher paper. This not only keeps their notes organized; it also provides an instant visual check on questions containing enough information and those requiring more research. Students can see quickly what information has already been covered, so they do not repeat themselves. Even though the group may choose to divide tasks at the beginning, they can reallocate labor later based on what their papers show them.

Originally, I thought of this as simply a notetaking activity. I now realize that it really supports cooperative learning by enabling groups to work together effectively. And it's wonderful for kinesthetic learners. Students who do not enjoy sitting for long periods do not have to; they often intuitively position themselves some distance from their papers so they can get the movement they crave. This makes it easier for them to stay completely focused on their reading and writing when they are in their seats.

Personal Response Notebooks

When students become experienced notetakers and have mastered the basics, using a format that encourages them to respond to the information in their notes helps them become more reflective notetakers (Stripling and Pitts 1988, 118). Now you are no longer just hoping they will follow Step 7 in the notetaking process.

Either a small spiral notebook or a section in a loose-leaf binder will work. Students take notes on the left-hand pages and use the margin to record the source and page number. On the right-hand side they record questions about their notes along with their reactions to them. Not every note will merit a response, and requiring one is an instant way to kill enthusiasm. You can make sure that students reflect as they gather information by requiring at least one response after every day of notetaking. Sentence starters can help those who insist they cannot think of anything to say. Try these: This is the most surprising thing I have learned because . . . I need to know more about . . . I also want to find out . . . I am interested in this because . . . This reminds me of . . . This is like something in my own life . . . I wish I could ask. . . .

This format works well with complex or controversial issues when you want students to think deeply about their topics. I have seen personal response notebooks on environmental topics that reflect anguish and involvement as students struggle with issues that often leave governments tied in knots. The subject need not be profound. The personal nature of biography is tailor-made for a response—I admire this; I can't imagine how I would have dealt with that; this person's life is so similar to or different from mine. Considering Michelangelo's life, a student commented, "He was lucky to live in a time when people valued art." This student was engaged. And talk about higher-level thinking. He had compared and contrasted Michelangelo's society with his own and made an inference.

ASSESSMENT OF STUDENTS' NOTES

When I began teaching notetaking, it made sense that I should also grade students' notes. I would get some good feedback on how well my students had learned and how I might want to change my teaching in the future. But when I sat down to look at those first notes folders, I found myself stumped. What exactly was I looking for? If I was not sure, how on earth could my students be? I made a list of grading criteria (see Fig. 9.5, p. 113) and vowed that from then on I would staple the criteria to the students' notes folders and review them during the research. Out of this first catastrophe evolved a fundamental rule—publish and share with students all assessment criteria both for the process and for the product.

Fig. 9.5. Criteria for Grading Research Notes

1. Information from <u>four</u> different sources, with majority of information <u>not</u> from a single source

2. Four bibliography cards

3. Note cards "keyed" to sources

4. Notes help answer researcher's questions. No irrelevant information

5. Adequate information for <u>all three questions</u>

6. Notes summarized

7. Notes in own words

8. One main idea (with supporting details) per note card

9. Sufficient quantity—*number will vary with assignments*

10. No glaring inaccuracies; double-check facts, especially numbers

I still grade notes for some student projects. It is a major time commitment, and I would not survive if I did it for all research assignments. Over time, some teachers have adopted my criteria for good notes. They are willing to spend time evaluating students' notes because they believe this leads to better final products. The eighth-grade social studies teachers at my school have developed common notes assessment criteria for a major project (see Fig. 14.5, p. 189), and they grade students' notes not once but three times during the project.

I also use a simpler process assessment for feedback only. It is especially useful when I am working with beginning notetakers. Early in their notetaking, students submit a single note card. I use these notes to identify struggling students who will require extra coaching. If many students are having difficulty with a common problem, for example, identifying supporting details, I will reteach the skill in a mini-lesson.

USING NOTES TO CREATE A FINAL PRODUCT

I still remember the sinking feeling I had the first time I discovered a completed project that had nothing to do with a student's notes. The style was dry, the vocabulary well beyond the average middle school student. Her notes had been excellent; this obvious copy was dreadful. I realized that many of my students did not know how to use their notes. Until now, they had been recopying material that had been copied in the first place. I needed strategies that would guide students in using their notes to create an original product. Some writing process techniques provided the assistance my students needed.

Freewriting

Many students are adept at freewriting. The only rule is to keep their pens moving for an allotted period of time, perhaps fifteen minutes. In writing class this may be undirected, with students simply asked to write whatever comes to mind. Directed freewriting helps students clarify what they want to communicate about a topic. The speed, the time limit, and the lack of finality make freewriting very different from the dreaded task of constructing a first draft.

In this directed freewrite, students read over their notes, then put them aside. They write using any or all of these prompts. What did I learn that's new? What did I learn that's exciting? What seem to be the most important issues or problems associated with my topic? What is the most important "news" I want to share with my teacher and classmates? (Tchudi and Tchudi 1984)

A freewrite can yield all sorts of treasures, the most basic being a sense of purpose. Students can also use it to develop a web of their main ideas, then go back and cross-check their notes to see what they may have left out. They may need to add some things to their webs. However, they may have overlooked some things with good reason; they do not relate to the central point the student wishes to make. Students often discover at least one perfectly phrased sentence they wish to save. It could be just what they need for an introduction that captures a reader's interest, or a conclusion that has an emotional impact. The freewrite itself is ready for the recycle bin; it has served its purpose.

Dialectical Writing

Sometimes it is good to get an outside perspective. Dialectical writing helps students refine their summary statements. Side-by-side pages in a notebook work best; students fold both pages down the middle, making four columns. In the first column, they list all that is essential to their individual topics. Using one or several of their listed items, they write a summary statement in the second column, and then exchange notebooks with a partner. In the third column the partner responds to what he reads. Is it interesting? Are there things that are unclear? Does he have questions or a need for more information? Using this feedback, each student writes a new draft. Done well, this provides a focus for the final product.

Planning for a First Draft

Students should develop plans for the final product by using a web or an outline. They will use their notes to help them decide which question to deal with first and how to sequence the information related to that question. Here one of the virtues of note cards becomes clear as students move them around as in a great game of solitaire. When they have used notetaking forms, they often cut them apart at this point. When the final product is creative, such as a short story, students must decide which events in their stories allow them to present the information for each of their research questions.

Collaborating with Writing Teachers— The Best Strategy of All

Language arts instructors teach useful things such as constructing introductions and conclusions. They can be great partners. When possible, arrange for them to teach or reinforce these skills when students are working on a research project. If your writing program emphasizes the writer's voice, they can banish the idea that the word *I* is inappropriate when writing about research. The optimum situation is to have students draft and revise their research writing in language arts class. The language arts teacher can advise students who are struggling to write coherent sentences from summarized notes or well-constructed paragraphs from related notes.

A THREE-YEAR INSTRUCTIONAL PLAN

Teaching students how to take good notes is a complex and many-faceted process that cannot be accomplished in a single all-purpose lesson. When preparing for any research assignment, teacher-librarians and subject-matter teachers need to identify the strategies they will use to expand and improve students' notetaking abilities. The teacher-librarian, as the only person who will work with students for all three years, must also have an overall vision of how to develop notetaking skills during this time. If students do not know how to take notes, it will not matter how well designed other aspects of an assignment may be. The copy machine paradigm will prevail, and plagiarism will be the end result. When students are able to take good notes, they experience pleasure from their own mastery. They feel power; they are able to make sense of the information they find.

REFERENCES

Stripling, Barbara K., and Judy M. Pitts. 1988. *Brainstorms and blueprints: Teaching library research as a thinking process.* Englewood, CO: Libraries Unlimited. 117.

Tchudi, Susan, and Stephen Tchudi. 1984. *The young writer's handbook.* New York: Scribners. 112, 114.

HANDOUT 9.1

NOTETAKING FORM

Name: _____

Big Topic: [   ]   Group: _____

CHAPTER 10

Reading for Information

Making Meaning

High standards were at the heart of the state's education reform efforts. Teachers, administrators, parents, and members of the business community had all been involved in the development of these standards. The department of education had sponsored in-service classes and funded local efforts to improve instruction. The next step involved testing students to see if they possessed the skills to meet the new standards.

The tests themselves would be different; they would not be normed. Instead of comparing students to each other to determine who was above or below average, these tests would determine who was able to meet the new standards and who was not. The first scores were a shock. In math, only about a quarter of the students were able to meet the standards. Reading looked relatively good with 48 percent at or above the standards, but this still meant that more than half the students had failed to meet them.

When state administrators met with parent groups and the media, they declared that the tests' initial function was to identify areas where instruction needed improvement. As changes were implemented, they believed scores would rise. Analysis of the reading tests identified a major problem area. Students overall were competent readers of literature; they could comprehend and respond intelligently to fiction and poetry. However, when asked to read nonfiction, they did not bring the same level of comfort and skill to the task. They had difficulty making sense of information.

REFORMING THE TEACHING OF READING

Most of the material read by adults requires them to make sense of information. Business representatives had urged that skills needed for reading information be included in the state standards. In theory, no one could disagree. In practice, most reading and language arts teachers continued to focus almost exclusively on literature. Although this story outlines the experience of a single state, there is no reason to believe it is not representative.

The Reading Teacher's View

Most language arts teachers enter their field because they love literature. They hope to transmit their enthusiasm to their students because they believe, and rightly, that a life without literature is an impoverished one. Over the years, these teachers have developed many activities to help students understand and enjoy stories, novels, and poetry.

These activities, based on such elements as character, plot, setting, metaphor, and simile, are rarely applicable to the reading of nonfiction. Thus, even during units when students are free to choose their own reading materials, those who select books on castles or dinosaurs or the history of surgery are often sent trudging back to the library because their books are the "wrong kind." Their teachers are often reluctant to accept nonfiction choices because they know these books will not fit in with planned activities focusing on such things as character and plot. Some reading teachers also reject nonfiction because they believe that most nonfiction for middle school students is of poor quality.

The Teacher-Librarian's Role

Librarians, as a rule, also love literature. But we are in a position to know exactly how much excellent nonfiction is being published for young readers. We must promote the best writing across the board, which means putting language arts and reading teachers in touch with outstanding nonfiction, too. Teachers will be more likely to use nonfiction if they find it appealing. Their students will be more likely to master skills for reading information when they practice using high-quality materials. Later, they may have to apply these skills to writing that is as dry as dust and dull as dishwater, but they should begin with well-written, high interest resources.

Librarians also know firsthand that many students struggle when reading for information. It is in our best interest to collaborate with teachers in delivering a program that gives students a solid grounding in strategies for reading nonfiction. This includes helping teachers identify needed reading strategies, assisting in the development of activities for teaching those strategies, and locating materials for use with the activities.

IDENTIFYING STRATEGIES FOR READING NONFICTION

When I first realized that my students needed strategies for reading nonfiction, I was unclear about precisely what they needed to know. My breakthrough came when I sat down one day to read a magazine article. I soon realized I had to work hard to understand what I was reading. "Aha!" I thought, "What if I do a task analysis? I'll watch myself closely and figure out exactly what I'm doing." I grabbed a pad and jotted down every strategy I noticed myself using to understand and judge the information in the article. (See Chapter 2 for more information on how to do a task analysis.)

When I was finished, I had ten different items. I was so excited that I grabbed an article on the economy I had been meaning to read but had kept putting off because I knew it would be slow going. I knew that my task analysis would work better with challenging reading. If the first article had been easier, I might not have used so many techniques, or I might have used them so unconsciously that they would have been hard to notice and identify.

After reading several articles, I had a long list of strategies. When I studied them to see if I could group similar approaches I identified four basic categories (Rankin 1992).

Judging Suitability

Most models of the research process tend to pair the selection of sources with the location phase, and certainly many aspects of selection do fall there—decisions such as: Are periodicals or on-line databases necessary for currency? Will primary sources be useful? Will special reference formats like chronologies or collections of statistics be required? Students will also choose or reject sources depending on whether they answer research questions, provide current information, and are written at an appropriate reading level.

The selection process often carries over into the stage of information processing. As students begin to read, they should make judgments about the suitability of a source in light of the background and preparation they bring to that source. If we do not teach students that they can abandon a source because they do not have the background to understand it, we actually encourage them to blunder along with totally inappropriate material.

The first problem I encountered when I sat down to read my challenging article was an unfamiliar word. Who among us has not found a student sitting baffled before a book that would challenge a graduate student's vocabulary? Whenever students will be researching in an area that is likely to contain some specialized language, it is a good idea to remind them of the usefulness of the dictionary, perhaps even some specialized dictionaries. Give a class permission to reject a source that is full of baffling words. Then a student can, with a clear conscience, put bewildering books back on the shelves and skip the Web sites written for specialists.

Students also need permission to reject, or at least postpone, a source at the wrong informational level. As I read my article, I found I had to ask whether I should continue when the author referred to some scientists with whom I was unfamiliar. What happens when a researcher comes upon the "Intolerable Acts" and has no idea what they were? What happens when another finds the country of Malawi mentioned and realizes that she does not even know the continent on which it is located? More than likely, both will continue on blindly unless we make it clear that it is important to fill in these informational blanks—usually by finding a brief overview in a reference book.

What if a writer assumes readers already have extensive knowledge of a topic? After two days of reading, a student wrote in his journal, "I've read a lot about the Long March, but I still don't get it. I can't figure out what the Long March was." He had begun his research with a very sophisticated book, and he had no real background on this period in Chinese history. After being directed to more basic reading, he noted later that his original book was finally making sense.

Just as some students will continue plodding through a book when they do not have the background needed to understand it, others may fail to recognize when they should move on to more complex information. Their journal entries often sound like this: "I read another encyclopedia article about my topic and didn't learn anything new." We must teach students to consider whether a source is written at the right informational level for them.

Finally, in the area of judging suitability, it helps to be aware of one's own style and to select sources that match one's strengths. A student who needs concrete examples should select different resources from another who feels at home with abstract theory. When a young learner knows that a picture is worth a thousand words, she should search for all the visual representations she can find. A slow reader should understand that if a source is too long, he will never finish it.

Handout 10.1, p. 127, summarizes student questions for judging suitability.

Understanding and Comprehending

After researchers select a suitable resource, they will want to employ a whole range of strategies for understanding it. There may be concepts they find confusing—what does inflation *really* mean? It is important to encourage readers to put on the brakes. Concrete learners may find it worthwhile to think of a real example for each idea they struggle with. If students can express an idea in their own words, either by explaining it to a friend, or writing it down, they can reassure themselves that they understand it.

Sometimes slowing down or even stopping is not enough; it's necessary to shift into reverse. In my economics article, the author kept referring to "economic terrorists," and I realized I was not sure what he meant. Simply plowing ahead through the article had not cleared up the mystery; it was time to go back to the place where the term was first introduced to see if I could find a definition or a clarifying example.

Another signal that it is time to backtrack comes when a reader must admit that she has stopped understanding what she is reading altogether—and probably has not been understanding anything for a while. Most adult readers have learned to retrace their steps to the point where they became lost and to try again more slowly and carefully. Middle school students are just as likely to keep reading, probably copying every bewildering word as they go. Or they may give up immediately in despair, possibly switching to some activity unrelated to their research to distract themselves from their frustration.

Although it is important to teach students to slow down, and even to shift into reverse when understanding eludes them, it is also necessary to teach strategies that will keep them on track. One of the simplest involves looking for signposts that indicate what will be talked about next. The sentence, "There are three central mistakes" signals what the author will be writing about. I noticed in my own reading that I wrote down some signposts, then checked them off as they appeared in the article. When students do this and find they have missed one, they can employ the now familiar trick of backtracking.

After reading, I automatically stopped to consider what the writer had wanted me to learn. Our students' understanding will also increase if they know how to identify major points. See Chapter 9 for an instructional strategy to use when teaching the identification of main ideas and supporting details.

We must also remind students to use visual information as an aid to comprehension. Visual information usually supports textual information in one of two basic ways—either by restating written ideas graphically or by making additional points not found in the text. Because more and more information in our society is communicated by way of visual images, we must work harder at helping our students make sense of visual information (see Chapter 12).

Handout 10.2 (p. 128), summarizes student questions for understanding and comprehending their reading.

Evaluating and Extracting Information

When extracting information from a source, the reader should constantly evaluate the usefulness of the information in that source. The "patchwork quilt" paper, in which a student stitches together unrelated scraps of information, is a pretty good indication that evaluation was not part of the extraction process. The "photocopy" paper, in which a student rehashes the truth according to the encyclopedia, is another. The first step in evaluating the usefulness of information is to decide what one wants from a particular source. A student who begins reading for any purpose other than an overview should be asking more than just "I would like to know something (really anything) about my topic." When I did my task analysis, I began my reading only with the desire to know more about economics and I quickly found myself floundering.

Given the sheer quantity of information available today, focused questions have become a survival skill for many adults (see Chapter 4). An environmentalist who often deals with two-inch thick government documents told me that she keeps asking: Do I need to read this section? Does this have anything to do with the questions I need answered?

It is not enough to help students generate questions at the beginning of a project; we must keep reminding them that their questions should guide their research. A bright eighth grader confessed that she was disappointed in her report on the Shakers. She had started out with excellent questions, but when she began to write her first draft, she realized that she had not answered any of them. "All I had was background," she sighed.

Students will be less likely to bypass their questions if they genuinely care about them, but since not every research project will be equally meaningful, we need other techniques that focus attention. Predicting what one expects to find in a source is particularly useful. If a student predicts that a tribe will have excellent hunting skills but no developed agriculture, he will read to verify his predictions. Having made some predictions, students will often be heard muttering, "Aha. I thought so," or "I didn't expect that."

As students progress in researching a particular topic, it is important that they fit their current reading into the context of what they have already learned. They should ask: Does this expand an idea? Does this make a completely new point? They need to be alert and ready to take action when something they read contradicts something they thought they knew.

Younger students, who have the idea that all nonfiction is "true," are often stymied when they find two contradictory statements in print. Facts are the easiest to deal with because we can teach students to double-check them in several other sources. Sometimes students learn that what they read in black and white is not as precise as they had thought; they often end up having to write a compromise statement like, "Estimates of the length of the Great Wall range from x to y miles." While this may be a fine way to approach an inanimate object like the Great Wall, opinions are more complicated. The critical thinking skills discussed in Chapter 8 should be employed to evaluate opinions.

Handout 10.3 (p. 129), summarizes student questions for evaluating and extracting information.

Following Up After Reading

When our source of information is another human being, we will usually ask that person to direct us to other sources—perhaps to books or to other people we can talk to. My task analysis showed me that I was going through the same follow-up procedure with my reading. Students can do this too by asking a few questions after reading. Does an author mention "authorities" on the subject? Does a book or article contain a bibliography?

We have all noticed the phenomenon of new information starting to present itself serendipitously once we become interested in a topic. We thought we were alone in our interest in this subject, but now it's a cover story in *Newsweek* and the focus of a television program tomorrow. Students should be on the alert for the sort of information that simply turns up without their actually searching for it. If they are lucky enough to notice new information, they can consider its similarities and differences in context with the things they have been reading.

Finally, information sources sometimes raise as many questions as they answer. Before parting company with a text, young researchers should routinely ask whether they have any new questions for which they will need answers.

Because I have discussed these four stages of using information sequentially, it would be easy to assume that one passes through them in this fashion; in fact, they will often happen simultaneously. As we work to understand a source, we may also be judging its suitability and/or evaluating and extracting information. However, there is a way in which the stages are "sequentially" interdependent. If we have not made a correct estimate of a source's suitability, we may find it too difficult to understand; if we cannot understand a source, we may find it impossible to extract information from it.

TEACHING STUDENTS TO READ NONFICTION

Strategies from the Four Basic Categories

With a little imagination and appropriate reading materials, most of the strategies detailed above will form the core of an activity. A paragraph containing unfamiliar and undefined words can be used for a lesson on looking up unknown words. Students should first be asked to try to make sense of their reading on their own. They can then compare their initial interpretation with their understanding of the paragraph after all the confusing words have been looked up. Such a lesson will prove especially useful if students will soon be reading materials that are likely to contain difficult vocabulary.

A short article containing a signpost statement—there are four causes, or two rules, or five reasons—can be used as students practice looking for those causes, rules, or reasons. Making predictions before reading is an activity students almost always enjoy, especially if the reading material is on an unfamiliar but intriguing topic, such as ironclads of the Civil War or mating rituals of penguins.

These sorts of lessons usually fit best into a full class period. They can be taught by a language arts teacher or a teacher in a particular discipline who wishes to prepare students for an upcoming assignment. On the other hand, students will have more interest in the strategies for evaluating the informational level of resources when the teacher-librarian presents them during an actual research project. Students can apply the strategies to the resources they locate. Similarly, the follow-up strategies that will lead a reader to new sources make more sense when presented in the midst of research.

If a strategy has been introduced in the classroom, the teacher-librarian may want to do a review whenever it seems relevant to a particular assignment. This is important when some time has elapsed since the strategy was last applied. It may also be necessary if the strategy was learned in a class other than the one where students will be doing research. Some techniques, like working backwards through a text one no longer understands, cannot be mentioned too often. The handouts at the end of this chapter can be used by students as checklists for assessing their use of any or all of the reading strategies.

Skimming and Scanning

Skimming and scanning are often mentioned in middle school, but rarely taught. Students need these skills to successfully apply many of the nonfiction reading strategies. If no one in your school teaches skimming and scanning, see if you can find some teachers willing to take ownership of these essential skills. You can do your part by introducing practice drills before research assignments likely to require the use of these skills.

Here is a warm-up that works well when students have to scan text for specific types of information. Find a short encyclopedia article on a topic similar to those the students will be researching. Condense that article to ten of the most interesting sentences and rearrange them so they are out of order. Place these on a student worksheet as ten separate sentences, each preceded by a short line. You will read the sentences in their original order, and students must find the sentence on the page and place the correct number next to it. The first sentence you read will obviously be number one. Timing your reading speed can be tricky. Watch students closely so that you do not go too fast. If students cannot keep up they will quit in frustration.

To practice skimming, give students five paragraphs on an interesting and concrete topic. Allow them one minute to skim the page. Then they must turn it over and summarize the main topics. You can increase the time if one minute is not enough. Skimming is also a component of the Brainstorm, Read, Categorize presearch found in Chapter 3.

Thinking Skills

One last word before we leave the teaching of nonfiction reading. Don't forget the thinking skills detailed in Chapter 11. Be sure to share them with reading teachers. They can be adapted to form the focus of engaging activities to use with nonfiction materials in a reading class. Some may also prove useful for making sense of textbook information in disciplines like social studies and science.

A PROGRAM TO PROMOTE QUALITY NONFICTION

The ultimate goal of a literature program is not just understanding, but enjoyment. Reading for pleasure should be part of a nonfiction reading program as well. More than a decade ago, while attending a children's literature conference, I realized that not only was I not promoting the best in nonfiction for young readers, I was not even buying it.

As I listened to one nonfiction author after another, I realized they chose topics that captured their interest. In fact, one could almost say the topics chose them. These were not writers who produced books on body systems or the states or drug abuse just because a publisher needed them. These were writers who wrote about their topics with enthusiasm, even passion. They did not use the language of encyclopedias. They were not afraid to say "I." They had a vision of young people reading their books and coming to share their interest and excitement. I knew I had to do something to connect these authors with middle school readers.

The people most willing to help me promote good nonfiction were my school's science teachers. They already used the library regularly; they believed reading and writing had an important place in the science curriculum; and they knew that many science books were a pleasure to read. We decided to inaugurate a program of science booktalks (Rankin 1988).

First, we had to acquire books worthy of booktalking, well-written books with a strong personal style. Since budget dollars were earmarked for materials to support the curriculum, we wrote a grant. Once we had a base collection of science books that could be read for pleasure, we would be able to supplement it each year through the regular budget. In purchasing books, I considered two criteria in addition to the quality of the writing. I needed a broad range of topics; there had to be something to interest everyone. I needed a range of reading levels, running from elementary to high school, to match the abilities of my students.

As the books arrived, I began to plan my booktalks. I never booktalk a fiction book I have not read, but I realized that I would not have time to read all of the science books I had purchased. And I did not need to. I read enough to get the flavor of each book, to find something exciting that I wanted to share, although some books were so irresistible that I found myself reading on and on.

The science teachers each looked for a vehicle to have students share what they read. They did not want to assign book reports; they remembered how they had hated writing them. One teacher asked students to design advertisements for their books. Another gave them the options of presenting a demonstration, of conducting an experiment, or of taking a survey. Still another had students write follow-up questions about things they still wanted to know about their individual topics. This proved a surprisingly popular assignment; some students were motivated to pursue answers long after the class had moved on to a different unit.

I learned to look for similar opportunities wherever I could find them. When a health teacher wanted students to read about health issues, I was able to come up with a selection of well-written books on everything from gangs to teen pregnancy. Students enjoyed using a comic book format to share what they learned. In my current school, the art teacher is an enthusiastic supporter of reading, so her students are able to read some of the outstanding art books written for young people. Where there is an interested teacher, a nonfiction booktalking program could just as easily fit into a history or geography class. When language arts students are working on voice, what better place to study the use of a strong personal voice than in quality nonfiction?

YOUR MISSION,
SHOULD YOU CHOOSE TO ACCEPT IT

Many students are poorly prepared for the reading they must do when conducting research. If they are unable to make sense of informational texts, then much of their research will be meaningless in the purest sense of the word. Teacher-librarians have a vested interest in changing this. We have a strong self-interest driving us, and this is good, because there will be many times when we will be met with resistance when we raise the issue. This mission takes patience.

Do not lose heart, though. We have two exciting secrets to share. Many excellent works of nonfiction for middle school readers exist. We stand ready to offer assistance with the perplexing task of teaching students to become skilled readers of nonfiction.

REFERENCES

Rankin, Virginia. 1992. Rx task analysis. *School Library Journal* 38 (November): 29–32.

———. 1988. Selling good science books. *Appraisal: Science Books for Young People* 21 (winter): 5–8.

HANDOUT 10.1

READING INFORMATION—
Judging Suitability

Name:_____

Is there confusing vocabulary?

1. A word I don't understand
   - find a definition
   - do I understand now?
   - look elsewhere for better definition?

2. Many words I don't understand
   - decide if language too difficult
   - if yes, choose another source

Is the informational level right for me?

1. Does it contain a few references to persons, places, or things I'm unfamiliar with?—Look for quick overview information.

2. Does it assume I already know *too many* things?—decide whether to:
   - keep reading and looking for quick information on each
   - read later in research

3. Does it mainly repeat what I already know?—Skim for new information, and move on to another source.

Does the writing style fit my reading style? For example, I may need concrete examples, or pictures, or short books.

HANDOUT
10.2

READING INFORMATION—
Understanding and Comprehending

Name:_____

Is a concept confusing? To see if I have it:

1. Come up with my own example

2. See if I can tell someone about it

3. See if I can write it in my own words

Are there terms the author keeps using that I'm not sure I understand?

Go back to where term was introduced, and look for concrete examples.

Do I feel like I've suddenly stopped understanding?

Go back through text to see where I became lost, and get back on track.

Use signposts to stay on track

1. Look for signs of what's coming, e.g., "There are 3 central mistakes: x, y, z"

2. Write them down

3. Check them off as they are explained
    - ask, "Where's y? Did I miss it?"
    - ask, "Is this y, or part of x?"

Can I sum up the main point?

1. Look at introduction and conclusion for clues

2. Look at topic sentences

3. Reread if necessary, skimming if possible

Are there visuals that also supply information? How do they relate to the text?

1. Restate written ideas graphically?

2. Make additional points not found in text?

HANDOUT 10.3

READING INFORMATION—
Evaluating and Extracting

Name:_____

Do I know what I want from this source?

1. Know the questions I want answered
   • keep asking if I need to understand *all* of this—does this section relate to my questions?
   • make value decisions—this is important; this is not

2. Make some guesses about things I expect to find, and look for them while reading

Am I making comparisons with what I have already read about this subject?

1. Does this expand an idea?

2. Does this make a completely new point?

3. Does this disagree with something I thought I knew?
   • if a fact, where can I double-check?
   • if an opinion, do I want to reconsider? reject?

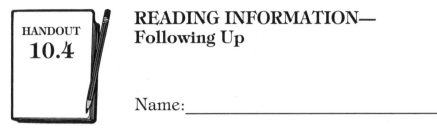

READING INFORMATION—
Following Up

Name:_____

Has the author mentioned other authorities on my topic?

    Should I try to find material by them?

Is there a bibliography that might give me ideas for further reading? I need to ask:

1. Which titles sound interesting?

2. Will I be able to find these materials in my school or public library?

After reading, do I notice my topic turning up in other places, like a television program, a conversation, the front page of the newspaper?

1. Keep my eyes and ears open

2. Ask how new information is similar to and different from what I've recently read.

Are there some new questions I have as a result of this reading?

1. Do I need to look for answers to them?

2. Where can I find answers?

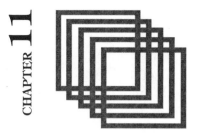

CHAPTER 11

Thinking Skills

Constructing Knowledge

One thing was clear from the start; my summer school professor was not sure I belonged in his class. "What's a librarian doing in a class on thinking?" My classmates, who appeared just as baffled, waited for my answer. Stunned, I managed to mumble that I believed research was a thinking process. In his class I hoped to discover strategies that would help my students become more thoughtful researchers. I'll show him, I thought, and I meant it quite literally. My class projects would demonstrate how thinking skills could be employed during the research process. I designed one unit employing the skill of evaluation to determine the usefulness of reference sources (see Chapter 8), and another applying the strategy of problem solving to the development of a research plan (see Chapter 5).

I began my exploration of thinking skills—by looking for opportunities to apply a specific skill to a specific step in the research process. When I began to search for ways to help students create quality products (Rankin 1996), I found myself going in a slightly different direction. In the final stages of the research process, as students prepared to communicate the results of their inquiry, I wanted them to "organize and analyze information in a new way" (Wisconsin Educational Media Association 1993), making inferences, drawing conclusions, and constructing meaning (Colorado Department of Education 1994). I realized there was a group of analytical thinking skills, more often taught in classrooms than in the library, that students could use to interpret their information and construct new meaning from it. These were skills such as sequencing, classifying, and decision making.

USING THINKING SKILLS TO ANALYZE INFORMATION

Everything we teach about the research process, from posing focused questions to taking summarized notes, is geared toward helping students construct new meaning from their research. Assessment criteria for final

131

products can also include, and indeed emphasize, original thinking. Requiring the use of a specific thinking skill as a lens through which students view their information is just one more piece of the puzzle. When we ask students to look at their research data for causes and effects, or to consider the pros and cons of competing solutions to a problem, or to sequence a series of events with an eye to determining the crucial turning points, we provide them with tools for making sense of their information and achieving new understanding.

Provide Structures for Using the Skills

My own thinking about thinking took a giant step forward when I began using PIE (Processing Information Environments; see Chapter 13). This approach involves planning research projects that include higher level thinking tasks. In my first efforts with PIE, I was able to design tasks that did indeed provoke quality thinking. But there were always some students who seemed confused and frustrated—uncertain what to do or how to do it.

I was ready for another step forward when I took a class with Nancy Skerritt and Emilie Hard of the Tahoma School District in Maple Valley, WA. I discovered two important techniques for structuring students' use of thinking skills. Graphic organizers provide a valuable visual framework to guide students as they apply a skill. Extension questions prompt students to draw conclusions about their information after they have used a graphic organizer. Without follow-up questions, the most thorough graphic organizer may still seem meaningless and merit no more than a "so what?"

I decided to apply what I had learned as I revised a speech writing task that was part of a Native Americans PIE. Students had to welcome a visitor to "their" tribes. Their speeches were to present vital information that would enable a modern time traveler to understand the people of the tribe and to live peacefully among them. After two weeks of research, some students identified so deeply with their tribes that the writing came easily. They automatically compared tribal culture with contemporary American culture, pointing out reassuring similarities and identifying possible pitfalls where differences were great. However, some groups always floundered

What if I did not leave the application of the needed thinking skill to chance? I decided to add an extra step by directing students to compare and contrast their tribal culture with contemporary American culture before writing their speeches. On a T-chart (see Fig. 11.1, p. 133), they could list the values, beliefs, and customs of both cultures, then use a Venn diagram (see Fig. 11.2, p. 133) to sort out commonalties and differences. To clarify their thinking, I posed a few extension questions. What important differences do you need to warn a stranger about? What unique aspects of the culture would a contemporary American find exciting or interesting? Are there some values or beliefs shared by the two cultures that might help a modern visitor feel more comfortable? Now everyone would be prepared to write that speech.

Fig. 11.1. T-Chart

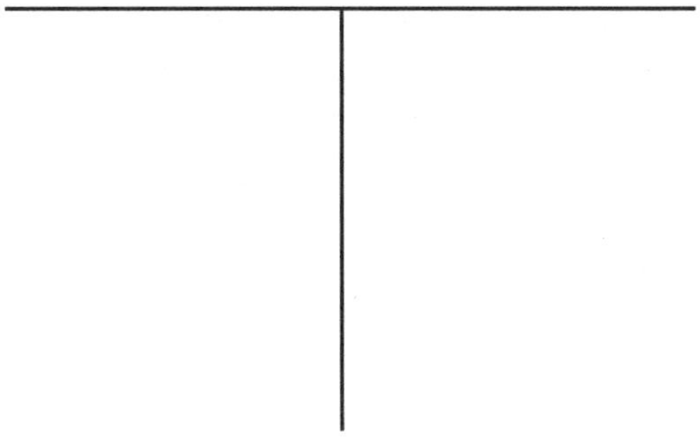

Fig. 11.2. Venn Diagram

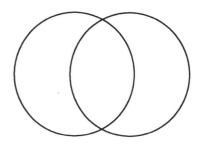

Once I had made this breakthrough, I saw opportunities everywhere for using thinking skills to help students analyze research information. Each time I asked students to apply a skill, I planned to provide a graphic organizer and extension questions.

Integrate the
Skills into Assignments

The thinking skills that will help students analyze information (see Fig. 11.3) are probably being taught somewhere in your school. Even if there is no formal thinking skills curriculum, many reading and language arts instructors now teach the skills as part of the study of literature. Much of contemporary reading instruction emphasizes that personal construction of meaning is necessary for comprehension. However, few teachers make the connection between these skills and library research. Your task is to find the teachers who are using thinking skills and make that connection for them. If thinking skills are truly overlooked in your school, try to integrate the skills into some likely assignments as a way of introducing them to teachers.

Fig. 11.3. Thinking Skills for Analyzing Information

- Sequencing

- Classifying

- Comparing and Contrasting

- Finding Causes and Effects

- Problem Solving

- Decision Making

Sequencing

When students research a historical topic, like the Battle of the Bulge, they can become lost in a succession of "and thens," unable to see the forest for the trees. When they consider a biographical subject, they may find themselves overwhelmed by such a welter of details that a writer's work as a bank cashier seems equal to the publication of his or her first novel. When they investigate a complicated process, like the making of a movie, they may not immediately see how script writing connects to editing or financing. Arranging events in order by applying the skill of sequencing can help.

A simple chain of squares linked by arrows serves as the graphic organizer for sequencing (see Fig. 11.4); if necessary this chain can snake back and forth across a page. How many squares you provide will depend on the complexity of the topic. Limiting both the size and number of squares forces students to become focused. They must summarize only the most crucial information in a small square. With a limited number of squares available, they will have to choose significant events; otherwise they risk detailing only the beginning of the battle, or the childhood of the writer, or the early days before a film is actually shot.

Fig. 11.4.

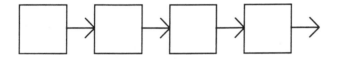

Extension questions will depend on the particular assignment, but here are some possibilities. What are three important turning points? How might things have been different if one event in the sequence had never happened? How does one event (you choose) relate to what came before it and what came after?

Classifying

Grouping things by common characteristics and then labeling them seems like a simple skill, but interesting possibilities for using it abound.

After researching famous painters, students list at least six words that describe the paintings of "their" artists. The words are then collected to make a class list. Small groups classify all the words on the list into categories, and the class then selects the most useful categories for discussing the work of painters. With luck, they will come up with all or most of the various perspectives from which paintings can be viewed—use of color, use of light, brush strokes, subject matter, etc. They are then ready to talk about the work of other artists.

Such an approach works well whenever a teacher wants students to draw some general conclusions from their individual investigations. After gathering information on various presidents, students might list the achievements of "their" president, then follow the same classifying procedure outlined for painters. In this case, the selected categories could lead to a class database listing presidents by their types of achievements—economic, military, territorial, diplomatic, political, etc. When I suggest categories, it is merely to indicate possible outcomes. For the categories to have meaning, students must label them with their own words. Extension questions include: What are the most common types of achievements? What are the most rare? Are certain achievements more common in specific time periods? Do some categories of achievements frequently occur together?

Classifying can be used effectively at the beginning of a project as well as at the end. Suppose students will soon begin research about colonial times for a newspaper. They can start by examining newspapers to identify categories of news stories—world, national, local, sports, style, food, weather, etc. Once a class agrees upon a list of categories, students use library resources to come up with possible story leads for each of the categories. Each newspaper group comes up with its own leads, and the editor then assigns his reporters to cover specific stories. If time is limited, this can be done more quickly when the teacher provides a list of story leads; students then work to classify them into newspaper categories. Extension questions before or after research will lead students to conclusions about colonial times. Which categories have the fewest leads, and what might the reasons for this be? Which categories lead to the most interesting stories? Which categories and/or stories would have been most interesting to a colonial person?

A basic web (see Fig. 9.3, p. 104) works well as a simple graphic organizer. Notetaking forms (see Handout 9.1, p. 116) can also help students sort out categories.

Comparing and Contrasting

After adding the skill of comparing and contrasting to the project on Native Americans, I realized that this skill would prove useful whenever students studied a different culture or country. Not only can they compare it to their own culture, they can work in pairs to share their information and compare the countries both students have researched. An extension question might require them to design a treaty that would capitalize on the countries' similarities or differences.

In addition to countries and cultures, comparing and contrasting helps students process information in such areas as planets, climates, endangered species, and minerals—all common middle school units of study. This skill is so widely useful that it's a good idea to laminate generously sized T-Charts and Venn Diagrams for repeated re-use with washable pens. Each unit will require its own extension questions if learners are to draw meaning from their charts and diagrams. Here is one more example. After comparing two minerals, choose one in which to invest a million dollars. In this case, students reach a conclusion by focusing on the differences.

Finding Causes and Effects

Most descriptions of historical events include some mention of causes and effects, but readers may either whiz right by them or never really comprehend them. Simple graphic organizers that are often used by sociologists (see Fig. 11.5) help young historians to focus on causes and effects and to select the most significant ones. By adding additional rings of arrows around the cause and effect circles, they can even identify causes of causes and effects of effects. An extension question might ask students to rank causes or effects in order of importance and then to explain their reasoning.

Fig. 11.5. Graphic Organizer for Causes and Effects

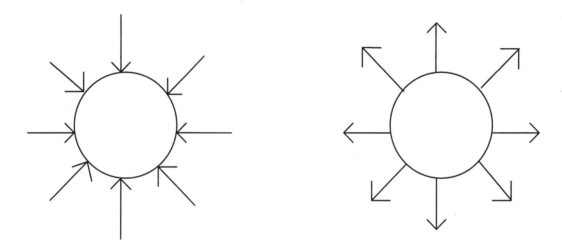

Looking at the causes and effects of environmental problems (such as deforestation) or social problems (such as youth gangs) helps to place these problems in a context. As coverage in these areas is more apt to be biased, you might ask students to analyze causes and effects from different points of view. How would a logger look at the causes and effects of deforestation? An environmentalist? An official of a third world country?

Students can follow a breaking news story, such as a major flood, over a considerable period, trying to discern causes and effects. Using the Internet in addition to a newspaper widens their ability to find data. Research in the library on floods helps them identify general causes and effects of floods and guides their investigation of the specific flood. Later they might compare the causes and effects elicited from the news coverage to the ones initially identified by library research.

Problem Solving and Decision Making

Although the four preceding thinking skills can be used together in a variety of combinations, they are quite distinct from one another. The lines between skills become blurred when we consider problem solving and decision making. A problem solver (see Fig. 11.6, p. 137) actually devises a plan or plans that may help resolve a problem (Beyer 1987, 26–28). A decision maker (see Fig. 11.7) identifies a number of options and chooses from among them (Beyer 1987, 29). But the problem solver will have to engage in decision making to choose the solution that holds the most promise, and a decision maker will frequently have to engage in problem solving to come up with the options from which to choose.

Fig. 11.6. Problem Solving

1. Define the problem. It may be helpful to:
   - break it into parts
   - identify causes
   - specify a goal

2. Devise plan(s) for solving the problem

3. Evaluate plan(s) using PMI (See Fig. 11.8, p. 138)

4. Choose a plan

5. If testing solutions, implement the plan

6. Evaluate and learn from implementation of the plan

7. Repeat steps 4-6 until an acceptable solution is found

Fig. 11.7. Decision Making

1. Specify goals to be achieved by the decision; the criteria for evaluation

2. Identify alternative options

3. Evaluate options using PMI (See Fig. 11.8, p. 138)

4. Rank options

5. Reevaluate the two or three highest options

6. Choose the best option

The type of problem solving applied in mathematics and laboratory science involves serial testing of solutions (see steps 4–6 in Fig. 11.6, p. 137). However, students using information gathered during library research will usually compare possible solutions and choose just one. When we eliminate serial testing of solutions, what remains is considerable overlap between the thinking skills of problem solving and decision making. Don't fret over these distinctions. Just know that sometimes it may be useful to focus on just one of these skills, but often the most effective strategy is a blending of the two.

When students research actual historical decisions, they will process their information on a higher level if they go through the decision-making process themselves. They can identify the hoped-for goals of the bombing of Hiroshima, or the founding of the League of Nations, or the Missouri Compromise. From a student's vantage point, these decisions may appear inevitable. Now we ask them to come up with other options for achieving the stated goals and choose the one that they think would have worked the best. History comes alive for students when they realize it is the story of real people who had goals and who made choices.

That realization is intensified by personalizing the choice and asking students to walk in the decision makers' shoes. After researching topics related to the Civil Rights Movement of the 1950s and 1960s, students are organized into small groups. Each group should reflect a range of topics: freedom rides, sit-ins, voter registration, school integration, mass demonstrations, marches, etc. Students report on their topics and the group evaluates each one as a tactic for ending discrimination by applying the PMI (see Fig. 11.8) strategy developed by Edward DeBono (Fogarty and Bellanca 1991, 234). An extension question asks students to imagine that they are young black people living during the period. Which strategy would they choose? Why?

Fig. 11.8. PMI

OPTIONS	PLUS	MINUS	INTRIGUING	RANK

If we want students to practice problem solving, schools themselves offer a wealth of problems needing solutions. Disaster preparedness (earthquakes, floods, etc.), weapons on campus, unappealing and/or unhealthy cafeteria food, use of drugs and alcohol at school, gangs, and sexual harassment are just a few. There may be a policy in place to deal with a problem, which may or may not be effective. Students begin their research with the policy, if one exists, and then move on to sources such as magazine articles and the Internet. Once possible solutions are identified, they should be shared with the school administration, student government, or a site-based council. The problem solvers can even conclude their presentations by teaching their audience the decision-making process.

Problem solving and decision making work just as well with assignments that have an element of fantasy as they do with those involving gritty reality. Take the popular assignment that obliges students to use research about a planet to invent an "alien" well adapted to living on that planet. Students go through the invention process as individual problem solvers, then meet with others who studied the same planet; they evaluate the options and make a decision on which alien is the best. As in real life, they may wish to combine elements from different plans. After the groups build their ideal aliens, they are able to introduce them to the class with a well-thought-out rationale for why they made the choices they did. It's even more fun to bring together two classes that have worked on the same assignment.

Pair Several Skills with a Single Assignment

Although problem solving and decision making form the most natural pairing, the other thinking skills can also be used in various combinations. Sequencing makes it easier to identify causes and effects, to say nothing of causes of causes and effects of effects. Finding causes and effects provides a context for problem solving. Classifying one's results after comparing and contrasting extends understanding. With the right topics, a teacher might be able to use all six skills. A teacher in my district once gleefully declared, "From two weeks of research, I get four weeks worth of information to use in my classroom."

If thinking skills are already being taught by subject matter teachers, your task is to show them how to integrate the skills into assignments. Identifying the right thinking skills for a specific assignment requires careful thinking. Some of my initial inspirations seemed brilliant, but they proved completely unworkable. It's wise to get a clear, step-by-step picture in your head of what students will be doing, and how you will prepare them to do it.

If thinking skills are not being taught in classrooms, it is a fairly simple matter for a teacher-librarian to introduce sequencing, classifying, finding causes and effects, and comparing and contrasting. After modeling how to use the skill with a graphic organizer, coach students as they practice applying the skill to analyze their research information. The more complex skills of problem solving and decision making must be taught in the classroom well before a research assignment, so that students have time to practice them in a variety of situations.

Make the Real-Life Connection

It also helps to practice applying the skills yourself—use typical research topics, newspaper articles, or your own life. As I helped my daughter apply problem solving to a life crisis, I suddenly understood the necessity of identifying several options. She had come up with a single solution, and the minuses clearly outweighed the plusses. I could see she planned to try her solution anyway. I insisted that she find at least two more options and evaluate them before deciding what to do. With only one option, her choice was a bad strategy or no strategy.

Thinking skills are extremely relevant in students' everyday lives, and you can help them make the connection through additional extension questions that focus on the learner rather than content. After they have practiced the skills in an academic context, we need to ask "personal" extension questions, such as: How can you use this skill in your own life? Why is this skill so important or valuable? In what kinds of situations have you seen others apply this skill? In what kinds of situations do you wish others had applied this skill?

Imagine a school where students analyze the plusses and minuses of a number of options before attempting to solve a problem, be it a personal problem or a learning problem. Imagine a school where students pause to look for the causes of a conflict with a teacher, or another student, as a strategy for finding a resolution to that conflict. Imagine a school where students sequence all the tasks and sub-tasks involved in a large project and then develop a plan to complete the project. Imagine a school where students make decisions carefully, not impulsively.

THINKING BEHAVIORS

Imagine, too, a school where students persist rather than quit when a solution to a problem evades them; where students show flexibility while working in a cooperative group; where students exhibit empathy as they try to understand another point of view; where students take risks to develop genuinely original products. The final, necessary piece of the thinking skills puzzle involves the teaching and reinforcing of thinking behaviors. Costa (1991, 19) has defined thinking behaviors as "those dispositions, attitudes, or inclinations that are characteristic of intelligently behaving human beings." These behaviors are demonstrated "when we are confronted with questions and problems for which we don't know the immediate answer." In identifying thinking behaviors, as with thinking skills, intelligent minds may differ. Costa (1991, 19–30), and Fogarty and Bellanca (1991, 180) present overlapping, but not identical lists of thinking behaviors. Figure 11.9, p. 141 represents a selection of behaviors relevant to thoughtful researching.

Fig. 11.9. Thinking Behaviors

1. Persistence—tries to complete a task; doesn't give up easily

2. Reflectiveness—thinks before acting; tries to control impulsiveness

3. Empathy—listens to others with sensitivity and understanding; puts aside judgments

4. Metacognition—considers and explains personal thinking processes

5. Precision—strives for accuracy and craftsmanship

6. Inquisitiveness—asks questions and identifies problems independently

7. Risk taking—goes beyond established limits; accepts the possibility of failure

8. Flexibility—considers alternatives; open to different possibilities

9. Originality—creates unique solutions to problems

Opportunities for Teaching the Behaviors

Although thinking behaviors can certainly be taught by teachers acting individually, a schoolwide approach that focuses on a different behavior each month is more effective. When everyone shares the vocabulary of thinking behaviors, there will be opportunities to connect them to different disciplines, and to the daily life of the school. If your school has advisory classes, they may prove the ideal place to introduce the "behavior of the month." Language arts classes offer another excellent forum for students to become acquainted with thinking behaviors. Short stories or picture books can provide powerful examples of the behaviors in action. Sometimes, social studies classes may afford the best conditions for presenting thinking behaviors. The only real requirement for a schoolwide program is that behaviors be introduced in a class every student takes.

Students will need to begin with a clear definition of the thinking behavior, plus examples of what that behavior looks like and sounds like. Adding examples of real people who typically display this behavior makes understanding even more concrete. Students can demonstrate their understanding of the behavior by designing posters that "sell" the behavior. Displaying the posters in halls and classrooms focuses attention on the behavior currently being emphasized; an "archival" gallery helps everyone remember the behaviors of months past.

A monthly faculty brainstorming session prior to the introduction of a new behavior aids teachers in identifying curricular tie-ins. Here are the kinds of things that may emerge: Social studies teachers conclude that empathy fits perfectly with an upcoming multicultural unit. Science teachers are sure precision serves students well as they work on science fair experiments. The health teacher realizes that persistence connects beautifully to the search for a cure for AIDS. The art teacher decides this is the perfect month for her most challenging project, one that definitely calls for risk taking. Toward the end of the year, when almost all the behaviors have been introduced, two language arts teachers have an exciting idea. They plan to ask students doing biographical research to identify the thinking behaviors most frequently displayed by the individual each is studying.

As you read this, you are probably thinking one of two things: This sounds great, but nobody in my school has ever heard of thinking behaviors; or people in my school teach thinking behaviors, but in an uncoordinated way. If the former is your thought, you can attempt to change things; recruit a few like-minded souls to form a committee with you. If the latter describes your school, you can try to convince everyone that a more coordinated approach will work better. Failing that, you can work with individual teachers to link thinking behaviors to specific research assignments. If none of these solutions will work for you, use the problem-solving strategy (see Fig. 11.6, p. 137) to develop three possible options that fit your situation.

Reinforcing Thinking Behaviors

Every time a student asks a clarifying question and we say, "I'm pleased with the inquisitiveness you have just displayed," we offer our students models of what the behavior looks and sounds like. When we say, "I am impressed with your persistence in working on this difficult assignment," we indicate that we truly value this behavior. In addition to this informal reinforcement, we can recognize students who employ thinking behaviors in more public forums such as the daily announcements, the school newscast, the student paper, the PTA newsletter. As thinking behaviors become an integral part of the daily conversation at school, students begin to realize that they have a range of options for responding to both learning and social problems. Their choices have been expanded.

Thinking behaviors can also be reinforced with extrinsic rewards. Most schools have some sort of reward system. In many schools, students who do something positive receive a ticket that is placed in a drawing for prizes. Selecting exemplary students as "Students of the Month" is another popular program. I have participated in both systems and find they work best when we define the behavior we want to reward. Linking thinking behaviors with a reward system offers a perfect way to highlight and reward one thinking behavior a month.

PREPARING LIFE-LONG LEARNERS

Thinking skills and thinking behaviors give students the tools they need to become life-long learners. As teacher-librarians committed to the achievement of this vision, we provide support and resources for others as they teach the skills and behaviors, we teach them occasionally ourselves, we help teachers connect them to research assignments, and we coach students as they apply them to those assignments. If we do these things and do them well, we can look forward to the time when no one will wonder why a librarian is interested in thinking skills.

REFERENCES

Beyer, Barry K. 1987. *Practical strategies for the teaching of thinking.* Boston: Allyn & Bacon.

Colorado Department of Education (CDE). 1994. *Information literacy guidelines.* Denver, CO: Colorado Department of Education.

Costa, Arthur L. 1991. *The School as a home for the mind.* Andover, MA: Skylight Publishing.

Fogarty, Robin, and James Bellanca. 1991. *Patterns for thinking. Patterns for transfer: A cooperative team approach for critical and creative thinking in the classroom.* Tucson, AZ: Zephyr Press.

Rankin, Virginia. 1996. Get smart: The crucial link between media specialists and A-plus student projects. *School Library Journal* 42 (August): 22–26.

Wisconsin Educational Media Association (WEMA). 1993. *Information problem-solving skills.* Madison, WI: Wisconsin Department of Public Instruction.

CHAPTER 12

Information in Visual Formats

The Eyes Have It

Victor loved his research topic, and he had worked hard on his project about the CIO. He knew that it was the "smash hit" of the first annual historical museum. The rotating CIO logo drew students to his display like a magnet, and, once there, they enjoyed pushing a button that caused tiny strikers to wave picket signs. Victor felt proud as he watched the crowds that gathered around his display.

The teacher-librarian's heart sank, though, as she listened to the students in those crowds. Most asked the same question: "What exactly *was* the CIO?" Victor certainly could have told them. He had tried his best to communicate what he knew. Indeed, he had covered three panels of cardboard with what amounted to a lengthy paper. He had tried his best to relieve the monotony with photocopied pictures of John L. Lewis and the sit-down strikers.

Later, when the teacher-librarian talked with Victor's social studies teacher, they both agreed that they had failed him, and his classmates, too. "Remember," they had told the class, "you are creating a museum, so you will need to communicate visually." With no specific guidance, the students had done their best, decorating their projects with bright colors, glitter, and sometimes even electric lights. The most creative ones had come up with unusual formats. Cupboard doors opened to reveal information about everyday life during the Depression. A boxing ring contained an account of Joe Louis's life. The exhibits were often eye-catching, but once the eye was caught, it was hard to glean much information without a significant amount of reading.

UNDERSTANDING THE
VISUAL DISPLAY OF INFORMATION

How does one communicate information visually? It was time to find out.

How to Learn More About Visual Formats

That first historical museum opened my eyes to a vast array of visual formats. They had been there all the time; I just hadn't noticed them. Well, I had noticed them—sort of. I knew they occurred with increasing frequency in newspapers and magazines, so I began my quest for understanding there. Now I would no longer simply notice visual presentations of information; I would collect them, categorize them, study them, dissect them. What were the different formats? What were the particular virtues of each? What techniques seemed to make a format most effective?

I started to clip good examples of visual communication. For a long time I did nothing but collect these examples. When I had a bulging folder of clippings, I decided it was time for some analysis. I sorted my clippings into basic categories such as maps, time lines, graphs. Then I sorted within the categories. Some maps provided information about locations. Some showed precisely where events had happened. Others linked numerical data to geographic areas. I looked at presentation techniques. Here color enhanced understanding; there it obscured it. One labeling method made information easy to comprehend; another left a viewer confused.

I naively thought that my first attempt at analysis would be sufficient. I now realize that I must work hard to keep up with the almost daily advances in visual techniques. My original collection of clippings looks a bit bland compared to the more complex examples I now find. Instead of just small boxes with data, I often find full-page pictorial displays combining a variety of visual schemes that connect and build on each other. I check my newspaper each day for fresh approaches to traditional formats.

Why Are Visual Displays Important?

Remember when pundits predicted that *USA Today*, with its emphasis on concise articles and colorful graphics, would probably fail in less than two years? Remember when the *New York Times* was completely black and white, and its visual displays almost exclusively grainy photographs? Take a look at the pages of the *Wall Street Journal* to recall a time when all newspapers expected subscribers to get their information through reading, lots and lots of reading. Even the *Journal* employs staff artists to design visual presentations such as the graphs that are a permanent feature on its front page. Check the *New York Times* and you will see that its artists receive a byline for particularly inventive displays. Both the *Times* and my local paper cite the information sources for their visuals with increasing frequency.

Computers have made this visual explosion possible. Information can be accessed and formatted at the speed a daily paper requires. Turn on the television, and you will see more visual techniques. Notice how annoying it is to watch a baseball telecast that does not include the tiny on-screen box crammed with information on the game. It includes the score, the count, the number of outs, the inning, and, most inspired of all, a diamond whose corners light up to indicate players on base (see Fig. 12.1). Who can imagine a Web site without visuals? And don't forget how increasingly pictorial nonfiction books for young people have become in the last decade.

Fig. 12.1.

All that glitters is not necessarily gold. Computer-generated graphics do not always combine substance with style; only a thoughtful, intelligent designer can do that. Graphics can oversimplify as easily as illuminate, manipulate as well as enlighten. We must prepare students to live in this world. They must understand basic principles underlying visual displays of information so that they can consider these displays with a thoughtful and critical eye.

Just as we teach our students to write as well as to read, so we must teach them not only to decipher the visual displays of others but to design their own visual presentations of information. We spend a dozen years working on their writing skills, but rarely do we focus on visual techniques. When we do require visuals with a project, we are often willing to accept the most bland, mundane work—clippings or photocopies with no information added. Visual products, such as posters, are often a hodge-podge of text and pictures with no discernible order or organization. We must teach high standards and apply them to the design of visual information. Students' creations must communicate information of substance and increase the viewer's understanding.

What Are Visual Displays Good For?

It is no accident that visual displays have become increasingly common in an information-rich world. They attract our attention more readily than blocks of text. They summarize and organize data, sometimes communicating so effectively that little further reading is necessary. When they arouse our curiosity, they may actually encourage us to read some of the initially daunting text.

Tufte (1990) points out that visual displays invite viewers to process information in their own ways. We need not all take the same path, as we do with text. I may start in one corner of a map, and you may choose another. I may initially notice intersecting points on a graph, whereas you may be drawn to the biggest differences. I may take a long time studying the individual parts, but you may immediately see a pattern. We are both actively engaged in making sense of and drawing conclusions about the information presented.

Designing a visual display requires the same sort of active engagement. Booth, Colomb and Williams (1995, 197–98) remark that this design work often extends and deepens a researcher's understanding. They suggest that attempting to arrange data in several different formats can highlight important patterns and relationships, and it can even lead to effective ways to organize the written component of a research project.

USEFUL VISUAL FORMATS

When we teach methods for creating visual displays, we are giving students tools first for understanding, and then for communicating information. Their knowledge of these techniques, and their experience in applying them, will also help them become more critical viewers of other's visual presentations.

Maps

Maps are a frequent component of research projects. In a student's mind, a map is often on a par with regurgitated information from an encyclopedia. One needs to find it and copy it. It is a task that requires no more thinking and analyzing than reproducing a country's flag or a state's official bird. When the student traces rather than photocopies a map, the task may have some value if he or she learns a bit about an area's geography in the process. When students look at each other's projects, they are likely to see copied maps as mere decoration and give them no more than a cursory glance. All this is unfortunate, because maps are marvelous vehicles for conveying information.

Maps That Provide Information About Locations

The most common function of a map is to show the locations of political entities, such as countries and cities, and/or physical features, such as rivers and mountains. Students can add information to a basic place map with a simple newspaper technique: text boxes. A local paper recently ran a map of Southeast Asian countries. The map was framed with small boxes of text detailing the status of Vietnamese refugees still living in camps in these countries. A narrow triangle extended from each text box and linked it to a specific country on the map. The writing in the text boxes was concise—an average of twenty words. A small but readable font was used.

Maps like these are easy to make. The map itself can be traced, purchased or photocopied. Text boxes can be connected to locations with yarn. Newspapers provide the best clues for use of color. Their maps use a few soft pastels; bright colors might distract from the story that is being told.

Few students escape middle school without having to do at least one research project about a country, and these projects almost always include a map. With text boxes, cities become far more than dots on the page (see Fig. 12.2). Text boxes explain that one dot represents the capital and seat of government; another the country's largest city and its economic center, yet another a major tourist attraction. Also identified are an important river and a rainforest.

Fig. 12.2. Location Map with Text Boxes

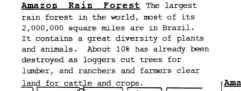

Amazon Rain Forest The largest rain forest in the world, most of its 2,000,000 square miles are in Brazil. It contains a great diversity of plants and animals. About 10% has already been destroyed as loggers cut trees for lumber, and ranchers and farmers clear land for cattle and crops.

Amazon River Really a network of 500 tributaries, it has the largest volume of water in the world Almost 4,000 miles long - only the Nile is longer. Fewer than 20,000 pureblooded Indians survive in the river basin.

Recife This commercial capital of the Northeast is called the "Venice of Brazil" because of the canals and rivers that crisscross the city. Narrow streets and houses recall the influence of the Dutch who settled here in the seventeenth century.

Brasilia The capital since 1960 and built especially for that purpose. It did not draw businesses and people from crowded coastal areas as had been hoped. The city is laid out in the shape of an airplane.

BRAZIL

Rio de Janeiro In a beautiful setting combining sea and mountains, it is a leading tourist destination in South America, a cultural center, and one of the world's great ports. Its population ranges from the very wealthy to the desperately poor who crowd into the slum dwellings that ring the city.

ATLANTIC
OCEAN

Sao Paulo Brazil's main business and manufacturing center is one of the world's fastest growing cities. It attracts many poor farmers from the countryside, and its diverse population includes people of Portuguese, Italian, Spanish, Lebanese, and Japanese background.

If the country is unfamiliar, text boxes will increase understanding of locations within its borders, but a viewer may still be unclear about its whereabouts on Earth. Another common newspaper technique can help. A small circle beside the map, with a box indicating where the map of Nicaragua would fit, places the country in its Central American context (see Fig. 12.3). A tiny map of the United States, with a particular state colored in, serves the same purpose, placing a state map in context.

Fig. 12.3. Location Map with Context Circle

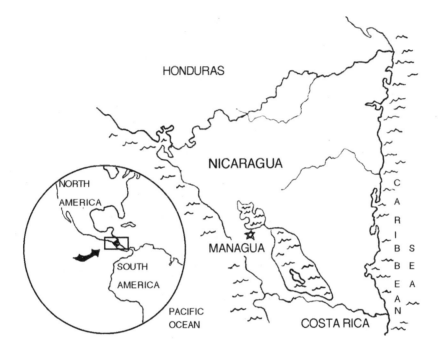

Such maps need not be limited to the social studies. Whenever geography is a component of a science topic, a map with text boxes can prove useful. Once Pacific Rim volcanoes have been located, text boxes can indicate whether they are active and when their last eruptions occurred. A map can show where specific endangered species still live; text boxes can provide details about their current status.

Maps That Link Events to Places

Newspapers also employ maps to show exactly where the events in a story happened. Text boxes surrounding a map of California detail recent flood damage. On a map of Russia, the text boxes are numbered so that readers may follow the route of a kidnapper in proper sequence. Newspaper maps focus on recent happenings, but this technique can also connect historical events to the places where they happened.

When a map is a required component of a historical project, students usually zero in on a single place. The Bonus March ended in Washington

DC, so one might just include a map of the nation's capital. But the veterans *marched* there—and sometimes took the train. How much more exciting to show where they came from and what towns they passed through, with text boxes revealing the story of organizers who traveled across the country from Portland, Oregon, picking up more and more participants along the way.

Similarly, a display relating how a family immigrated from Ireland will often merit no more than an unadorned map of Ireland. The family's story comes alive when a map uses text boxes to trace their travels. The map makes their odyssey real (see Fig. 12.4).

Fig. 12.4. Historical Map with Text Boxes

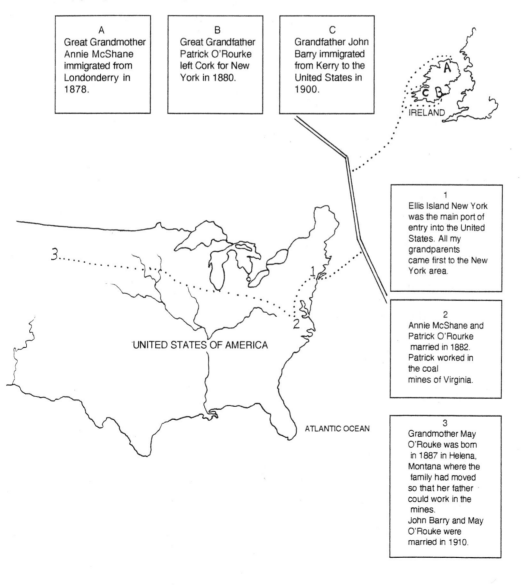

The O'Rourke and Barry Family Odyssey

In the late 1800s, people who did not own land could not marry in Ireland. This law was passed to prevent further subdivision of family owned property among the heirs. My great grandparents immigrated to the United States in order to have a full life.

> **A**
> Great Grandmother Annie McShane immigrated from Londonderry in 1878.

> **B**
> Great Grandfather Patrick O'Rourke left Cork for New York in 1880.

> **C**
> Grandfather John Barry immigrated from Kerry to the United States in 1900.

IRELAND

> **1**
> Ellis Island New York was the main port of entry into the United States. All my grandparents came first to the New York area.

> **2**
> Annie McShane and Patrick O'Rourke married in 1882. Patrick worked in the coal mines of Virginia.

> **3**
> Grandmother May O'Rouke was born in 1887 in Helena, Montana where the family had moved so that her father could work in the mines.
> John Barry and May O'Rouke were married in 1910.

UNITED STATES OF AMERICA

ATLANTIC OCEAN

Before designing their own maps, students can deepen their understanding by analyzing professionally prepared maps. Clip any good ones that you find in newspapers and magazines. When these maps are mounted and laminated, they can be used again and again in an exercise where students practice writing summary statements after examining the map and its text boxes.

A map of California's floods might lead a student to declare that the worst flooding happened in coastal areas in the southern part of the state. After reading all the information on the Russian kidnapping, a student might conclude that although the kidnapper wanted to reach Iran, he was able to travel only half the distance to that country's border. Neither the text boxes nor the map is sufficient on its own to lead students to a conclusion; they must look at both. You will be training students to carry on a dialogue with a map. They will ask, What can this map tell me? What can I deduce from it?

When students first use text boxes in their own map making, they should write a summary statement explaining what they are trying to communicate through their maps. Classmates can evaluate each other's work by deciding whether each map does communicate the message in the summary statement.

Maps That Display Data

Although atlases have used economic and thematic maps to display data for a long time, such maps are now used with increasing frequency in a variety of venues. Maps can instantly clarify regional patterns for such matters as poverty, unemployment, or crime rate. They have an impact that no list can match. Data maps make comparisons easy—here the per capita income is high, there low.

Before students design a map to display data, they must have a reason for doing it; they must have a story they wish to tell. Therefore, it makes sense to begin by studying data maps prepared by experts: maps presumably designed to make a point.

To demonstrate the potential of data maps, I always begin with an outstanding example. On a U.S. map from the 1970s, various shades of pink and blue make it clear that males outnumbered females west of the Mississippi, whereas the reverse was true in the eastern part of the country. The map demonstrates some design principles. There is a good reason for this map; there is a point to be made. The use of color supports the message, albeit the stereotyped pink for females and blue for males. However, the point could just as easily be made with shades of green and orange. The most important thing about the use of color is the simplicity and easy readability that occurs when only two colors are used.

I show several different types of examples. I do not want students producing only maps with two colors scaled from light to dark; they will not always be appropriate. A public health map indicating the ratio of physicians to population uses four bright colors. A quick glance at the key leads to the conclusion that California, New York, and southern New England have the most doctors per capita. One can also determine that many southern states have fewer doctors, and that most states seem to fall somewhere in between the two extremes. A few contrasting colors work well in this particular map, because differences tend to be regional; big blocks of color highlight this. If the data display had looked more like a checkerboard, one or two graded colors might have been easier to decipher.

A map with many colors may prove confusing if the colors have no logical association with the topic under study; eyes must repeatedly return to the key. On the other hand, rainbow-hued weather maps are easy to decipher because we can deduce that blue indicates a cold area and red means a hot spot.

Sometimes the data displayed on a map may be easy enough to understand, but still not make sense. A map showing the crime rate by states leaves a viewer asking how Washington and Oregon can possibly have higher rates than the more likely northeastern states. What kinds of crimes are we talking about? Does car theft have the same weight as murder? Where were these crimes more likely to happen—in urban areas or rural ones?

Reusable, laminated examples of such maps can again be used as a teaching tool, this time to help students deepen their understanding of data display. I supplement the ones I find in newspapers and magazines with pages harvested from outdated economic and thematic atlases. Students, working individually or in pairs, can examine these laminated maps and list the conclusions they are able to draw from the displays of data. Once again, we are encouraging the students to converse with the maps; later, when they design their own, students will understand the maps must contain enough information to make such conversation possible. At some point, you may also want them to critique the design and to decide whether or not it was effective.

Students can find data for their own maps through such sources as almanacs, *The Statistical Abstract*, the U.S. Bureau of the Census, and many other government departments. Adding color to simple outline maps will keep the emphasis on thinking rather than drawing. If a computer mapping program is used, make sure students stay focused on the information they wish to communicate, and ignore the siren call of glitz and special effects.

Graphs

Not all numerical data have a relationship to geography, and even when a relationship exists, a map may not always be the most effective way to display the data. Graphs offer an alternative. Unlike maps, graphs are not a typical requirement for a research project. However, once students are exposed to the possibilities of communicating numerical information through graphs, you may be surprised to discover how many opportunities they find to do so. You may also be surprised by the amount of numerical information contained in the books on your nonfiction shelves.

Line Graphs

Booth, Colomb, and Williams (1995, 178) suggest that a line graph is an excellent way to display data when you wish to hammer home a point, rather than invite readers to draw their own conclusions. A line, shooting up to indicate rising consumer debt, or plummeting down to track declining farm acreage, makes an immediate impact.

Tufte (1997, 103) notes that the parallelism of line graphs highlights contrasts and comparisons. Line graphs are often the best choice for showing changes over time. A quick glance at a graph comparing the unemployment rates for the United States and Canada tells me the U.S. rate used to be higher, but dipped below the Canadian rate in the late seventies. It stayed there through 1995, with the gap between the two countries widening (see Fig. 12.5). Just as a Venn diagram (see Fig. 11.2, p. 133) facilitates the task of comparing and contrasting verbal information, a line graph helps students compare numerical information.

Fig. 12.5. Line Graph for Comparing and Contrasting

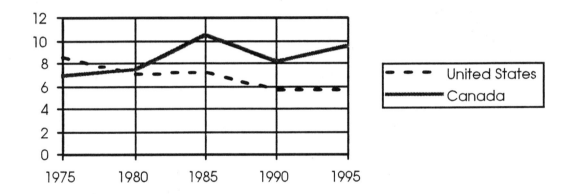

Bar Graphs

Bar graphs also highlight comparisons, and they make a good choice when changes over time are not particularly dramatic. In other words, the numbers will not yield a dramatic slope on a line graph.

One has a freer hand in determining the order of data when time is not one of the variables on a bar graph. Data can sometimes be arranged to produce the same attention-getting slope often found on a line graph. The bars representing literacy rates for a number of African countries go from lowest to highest (see Fig. 12.6, p. 155).

Although most line graphs look pretty similar, bar graphs are more varied. When collecting examples of graphs to use in teaching, I watch for particularly creative uses for them. Most student bar graphs will be simple, serviceable displays of data, but some outstanding examples can provide inspiration for divergent thinkers. These bar graphs will be unusual, perhaps even unique, and will communicate in a particularly effective way.

Fig. 12.6. Bar Graph for Making a Point.

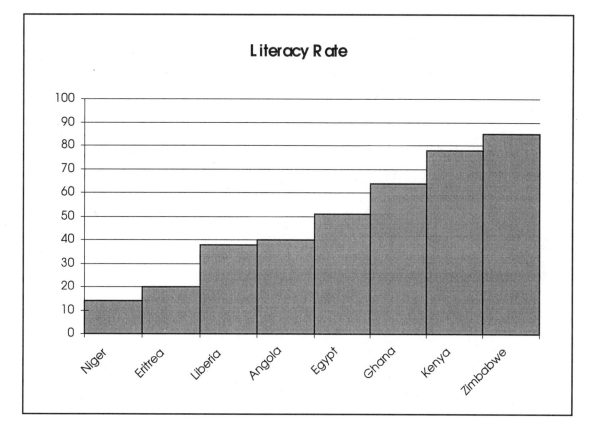

Consider three simple bars representing the years 1959, 1989, and 2010; each is divided into three parts. The top component, thin and black, always stays the same; it equals the top four percent of wage and salary earners in the United States. At the bottom of each bar is another black block, much thicker; it tells what percentage at the lower end of the population earned as much money as the top four percent. The shrinking white space, between the two blocks of black, powerfully illustrates the shrinking of the middle class over time (see Fig. 12.7, p. 156).

Bar graphs lend themselves to decoration, but beware those for which the design becomes so clever that it tends to obscure the data. The most creative bar graphs derive their power from an inspired simplicity that lends impact to the story the graph is telling. During a water shortage brought on by drought, one local paper featured a daily bar graph on water use. The first bar indicated the target rate of consumption, the second the actual rate, and the third the normal rate. Each day, the three bars communicated information more speedily and eloquently than could any words: not only was water use slightly below the target, it was substantially below the normal rate.

As with all the visual techniques in this chapter, you will want to provide opportunities for students to analyze professional examples, and then to design their own. After some practice with both types of graph, students can also consider whether specific data lends itself best to a line or bar graph.

Fig. 12.7.

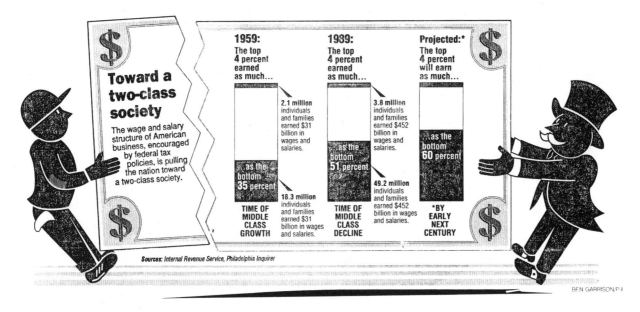

Sources: Internal Revenue Service, *Philadelphia Inquirer*. Reprinted with permission, *Seattle Post-Intelligencer*.

Tables

Graphs display no more than two variables, but sometimes a subject yields pertinent data in a variety of categories. When several graphs do not seem the best choice for conveying all this information, a table with data ordered in rows or columns can prove useful.

A bar graph displaying modem speeds, from poky old analog technology to the dazzlingly fast new cable modems, with everything in between, will definitely catch the eye of an Internet user. But wait. There are other questions to consider. How much does each type cost? Where and when will each be available? What type of equipment is required? An accompanying table allows a designer to display all this information. A viewer can make comparisons based on the categories most important to him or her. Speed may be the top priority for one individual, whereas another may want to consider cost first. Although such a table may seem complex in comparison to the graph, tables often convey information more effectively and concisely than blocks of text (Grossman 1993).

Tables invite thoughtful viewers to review data and arrive at their own understanding of the meaning of that data (Booth, Colomb, and Williams 1995, 179). Many conclusions can be drawn from a perusal of the data for Seattle weather (see Fig. 12.8, p. 158). June 1998 was obviously cooler than the average June; the temperature fell below the average high on 20 of 30 days. However, it never fell very far below; this is obviously not a place that experiences extreme weather. That conclusion is bolstered by the very modest changes in the average high and low temperatures. Whenever a student's data is extensive and readers need exact figures, a number table is the best choice (Booth, Colomb, and Williams 1995, 179).

Tables are extremely versatile; they can be used to display numbers or text, or, as in the case of the modems, some combination of the two. Middle school researchers will find tables useful for organizing information on a multifaceted topic, thus introducing their subject to others and inviting them to learn more.

Let's follow Ethan as he designs a text table for his poster, "My Family and the Military" (see Fig. 12.9, p. 159). Ethan's brother, father, uncles, grandfathers, and a great grandfather have all served in the armed forces. He worries that he has more information than he can fit on his poster or that his classmates will care to read. Using the thinking skill of classifying (see Chapter 11), he sorts his information on his relatives into categories: name, relationship to himself, branch of the service, highest rank achieved, wars and conflicts fought in. If he presents all these facts in a table, the rest of the poster will have enough space for a photograph of each man and a short anecdote about his experiences. Ethan is relieved, because the stories are the heart and soul of his project.

He has one more brainstorm; if he assigns a number to each man on the table, then numbers the photos and anecdotes as well, viewers will be able to move back and forth easily between his writing and the table. His final decision involves the order in which he will present the men—chronologically, of course—but should he start with his brother and dad, whom many of his classmates know, or his great-grandfathers and grandfathers, who fought in the World Wars so many students still find fascinating? He presents his choices to a few friends who all advise him to begin with the eldest.

Ethan went through some important steps for anyone designing a table. He sorted his information into categories. A table can present a good deal of information, but Ethan, with six categories and therefore six columns, had probably reached the limits of effective data display. In fact, his first table seemed too crowded to him, so he decided to indicate the branch of service in the column for rank. If he had identified more categories, he would have chosen the ones that seemed most important.

He also made some decisions about how to arrange his information. Since his project told a historical story, he used time as a major organizing element. He knew that the order in which he presented his categories would also have an impact. He reasoned that the wars in which the men fought would hold the most interest for viewers, so he chose to place that column on the right edge where it would stand out.

Fig. 12.8. Number Table—Seattle Weather, June 1998

Date	High	Low	Record High	Record Low	Normal High	Normal Low
1	62	51	94	40	67	49
2	72	52	94	40	67	50
3	66	51	87	42	67	50
4	60	53	88	41	68	50
5	66	53	92	41	68	50
6	75	52	84	42	68	50
7	79	51	87	42	68	50
8	67	54	87	43	68	51
9	64	54	96	44	68	51
10	59	53	83	43	69	51
11	71	54	84	40	69	52
12	72	52	82	38	69	52
13	66	50	90	42	69	52
14	62	48	86	43	70	52
15	61	48	88	43	70	52
16	67	48	88	42	70	52
17	64	49	91	43	70	52
18	60	50	94	43	70	52
19	65	50	92	43	71	53
20	74	50	86	43	71	53
21	82	54	89	43	71	53
22	69	53	92	45	71	53
23	67	54	92	40	71	53
24	62	51	92	45	72	53
25	63	52	87	45	72	53
26	63	52	88	46	72	53
27	69	52	85	45	72	54
28	77	53	91	45	72	54
29	82	54	93	45	73	54
30	75	53	96	43	73	54

Reprinted with permission, *Seattle Post-Intelligencer.*

Fig. 12.9. Text Table—My Family and the Military

Number on Display	Relationship	Final Rank	Name	Wars and Conflicts
1	Great-grandfather	Major (Army)	Willard Kendall	World War I
2	Great-grandfather	Private (Army)	Michael Donohue	World War I
3	Great-grandfather	Sergeant (Army)	Brian Moran	World War II
4	Grandfather	Captain (Army)	Arthur Kendall	World War II
5	Grandfather	Private (Army)	Patrick Donohue	Korean War
6	Uncle	Colonel (Air Force)	Richard Kendall	Korean War Vietnamese War
7	Father	First Lieutenant (Army)	Timothy Kendall	Vietnamese War
8	Uncle	Private (Army)	Brian Donohue	Died in Vietnamese War
9	Uncle	Sergeant (Army)	John Donohue	Vietnamese War
10	Brother	Ensign (Navy)	Brian Kendall	On alert in Persian gulf

Newspapers are full of tables these days; they appear to be one of the most popular ways to display information. A recent search for examples yielded a rich harvest. A numerical table compared actual rainfall for a one-week period to the record, average, and forecast. A text table concisely reviewed proposed solutions to the decline in local fisheries, showing each solution's current status, its chances for adoption, and groups likely to be impacted. The sports section produced a table that mixed text and numbers to describe the all-state high school basketball teams. Included were each player's position, school, height, statistics, and strengths.

Time Lines and Sequences

After maps, time lines are the visual devices most likely to be required for a project. As with maps, time lines are frequently copied directly from a source, usually after all notes have been taken. This copying may be necessary if a student's notes contain few dates. You can try warning students that they will need to include dates in their notes, or you can require them to take notes on a time line as they read. To take time line notes, they draw a line along the length of a sheet of paper, figure out the amount of time needed to complete their topics, and finally divide the line into an equal number of sections. Decades work well for biographical subjects; years, months, or days for historical events.

Student writers, given any sort of biographical subject, are likely to fall into an "and then" mode of writing, plodding along through childhood and youth and growing weary before they ever come to the achievements for which the person is remembered. Avoid this by requiring a time line to present important dates in the subject's life. Direct students to focus their writing on such issues of substance as early obstacles and advantages, motivations, important influences, accomplishments, failures, and lasting effects. Make sure the assessment criteria reinforce these requirements.

Newspaper chronologies rarely follow a horizontal time line format, but usually present events in paragraphs introduced by dates and ordered down a vertical column. One loses the patterns made clear when events are arranged along a line representing specific amounts of time, but one gains the space to write about each event in more detail (see Fig.12.10).

Fig. 12.10. Chronology of the Life of Joseph MacLean

♦ **1822:** Born in Edinburgh, Scotland to a desperately poor family with eight other children.

♦ **1835:** Runs away to sea seeking a better life.

♦ **1844:** On a voyage to the Indian Ocean, plague wipes out most of the crew. Joseph is one of the few who survives.

♦ **1848:** Gold is discovered in California.

♦ **1949:** Sails around the Horn to California to seek his fortune. He returns with $300,000.

♦ **1850:** Meets Albertine Marchais of Paris, France, in New York City. They marry after a brief courtship.

♦ **1851:** Returns alone to California, traveling overland across Panama. He reappears in New York City with $200,000.

♦ **1852:** Settles permanently in New York City and begins investing in real estate.

♦ **1862:** Birth of only child, Wilbur MacLean. Effects of childbirth leave Albertine an invalid for the rest of her life.

♦ **1872:** Albertine dies. Joseph, grief stricken, commissions the carving of an enormous stone angel for her grave in Cypress Hills Cemetery, Queens, NY.

♦ **1875:** Rheumatism grows extremely painful, but Joseph remains active, increasing his fortune through real estate investments.

♦ **1892:** Dies in New York City and is buried with Albertine.

Another way to show change over time is with an illustrated sequence. One of the best examples is a famous series of posters that begins with a small house in the country. In the following five or six pictures, more and more features—roads, buildings, signs—are added to the landscape. The house can barely be seen at all in the final, busy, urban panorama. Local history sites can be illustrated in this manner (see Fig.12.11) as well as changing environmental sites.

Fig. 12.11. Illustrated Sequence—Mayfield

Pictorial Representations

As the above example shows, a picture really can be worth a thousand words. Pictures supplemented with a few well-chosen words produce concrete and memorable explanations that tie together a number of related factors.

Explanations of Causes, Effects, Problems, and Solutions

A compact scene shows a factory with smokestacks belching pollutants; across the street a woman is burning some trash in her yard while a wood stove keeps her house warm; nearby, a man is filling his tank at a gas station. Each item sends up a smoke-like bubble containing an explanation of its impact on air pollution (see Fig. 12.12).

Fig. 12.12. Pictorial Representation—Solutions to Air Pollution

Imagine a snaking stream. Along its banks, we see a suburban development, dikes to keep water out of the flood plain, a dairy farm that sends a variety of pollutants into the stream, and a clear-cut slope that leads to increased flooding. Text boxes tell us how each of these things poses a danger to the fish in the river.

Both of these graphics will attract attention. They also clarify and connect information that might seem more confusing if presented exclusively through text. By actually picturing causes, effects, problems, and solutions, this information will remain in the reader's memory long after viewing.

Transformations of a Static Topic into a Dynamic Narrative

Information on a plant will certainly be enhanced by a high-quality botanical drawing. An illustration in *Visual Explanations* (Tufte 1997, 126) shows how lively such a drawing can become when information that is usually presented textually is added to the picture. A drawing of "the ultimate weed," an imaginary creation, shows more than just the expected root, stalk, leaves, and blossoms. We see the seeds blowing off into the air; in a den near the roots, a rodent lies dead from eating this toxic plant; ranged along the ground are seedlings that grow very rapidly; a profile with runny eyes and nose indicates the plant is an allergen. This is just a fraction of the pictorial information in this picture, all of it made clear by the addition of only 41 words.

Tufte (1997, 126) tells us that the difference between the drawing of the ultimate weed and a standard botanical illustration is that it portrays verbs as well as nouns. Notice how lively and memorable the information on bears becomes when given this treatment (see Fig 12.13, p. 164). The principle can be applied to many illustrations that might ordinarily merit the caption, "Parts of a . . . ." Drawings of inventions, for example, can often benefit from the addition of illustrations based on verbs. The verbs help us place the illustrated subject, whether living or inanimate, in a context.

A pictorial representation is the only visual format presented in this chapter that requires actual artistic talent. For students who possess such a talent, designing a pictorial display of information offers a much more creative outlet than mere copying. Even so, the artistic merit of an illustration must be matched by the power of the ideas underlying it. Only students who can take textual information, and imagine how they might illustrate it, will be able to use this technique.

Text As a Visual

The headline is probably the most familiar example of text used to make a visual impact. Let's return to that museum exhibit on the CIO to see how some text-based techniques might have helped students answer the question, "What exactly was the CIO?"

Fig. 12.13. Dynamic Narrative of a Bear's Life

Summary Boxes

Suppose Victor had written a concise statement that answered this question. If he had then placed the statement in the center of his display, students would have noticed it and begun their exploration of his project with this basic information. Just to be sure everyone noticed it, he would have typed his statement using a large type face, 24 to 28 point. He might also have added a border or printed his statement on colored paper. Figure 12.14 contains an example of a summary box.

Fig. 12.14. Summary Box

In 1848, when gold was discovered in California, many young men decided to go West in search of a possible fortune. A young Scottish immigrant named Joseph MacLean, my great-great-great-great-grandfather, was one of these original Forty Niners. The lives of these miners were very hard, and few made any money at all. Joseph was lucky. He came away with a half million dollars. I will tell you what I have learned about him, and about the lives of the Forty Niners in the Great California Gold Rush.

Before beginning research for the historical museum, students now receive a product assessment sheet (see Fig. 14.4, p. 188). It identifies a summary box as a required element and explains its purpose. "Contains a Summary Box—brief overview of topic in paragraph form that draws in the reader and states a clear central purpose for the whole display." Students are given time in class for a dialectical writing exercise (see Chapter 9) to help them identify the information to include in their summary statements.

Highlights Boxes

Students begin their dialectical writing by listing everything they believe to be important about their topics. By the end, they should have a focus, a clear central purpose for the display. They may still be able to use many of the items they placed on their initial lists. The assessment sheet also indicates that a highlights box will be required, and that it must present the major points of the display "with bullets."

Students learn what makes a good highlights box by viewing slides and posters. Examples, clipped from news stories, make clear that a highlights box is not a table of contents. Included are boxes detailing the major features of a piece of legislation, the key points in a treaty, and the issues that led a union to strike. When a young researcher encounters difficulty identifying the highlights of his or her topic, writing brief answers to the questions embodied in the "Five W's and an H" may help (see Fig. 12.15 and Chapter 4). Those who do nothing more than read the summary statement and highlights box for a display should come away with a basic understanding of a topic.

Fig. 12.15. Highlights Box

WHO: At least 250,000 people went to California during the first five years after gold was discovered. Ninety percent were men. California's population grew from 15,000 to 100,00 by 1849, and San Francisco was transformed from a small town to a city of 25,000.

WHAT: This was the first true gold rush—an enormous migration of people seeking gold. The California Gold Rush stimulated shipping, commerce, manufacturing, and farming.

WHERE: The Forty Niners came from the United States, Mexico, China, and South America. They traveled by land across Panama, Nicaragua, and Mexico, then by boat up the Pacific Coast. Others traveled by boat around Cape Horn, South America. Ships docked at San Francisco, where travelers took smaller boats up the Sacramento River. Many people also took the California Trail from Nebraska to California. Everyone's destination was the western slope of the Sierra Nevada Mountains.

WHEN: Gold was discovered at Sutter's Mill on January 24, 1848. The peak Gold Rush years were 1849--1854. Many mines were exhausted by the late 1850s.

WHY: Many poor and ordinary people hoped to get rich overnight. In the end, more merchants became wealthy than miners.

HOW: Miners sifted gold from the gravel in stream beds by swirling it in small pans or rocking it in larger boxes. Motion brought the lighter material to the top while gold sunk to the bottom.

Quotation Boxes

A quotation box should make a reader want to know more. No one can limit their knowledge of the CIO to the summary and highlights boxes when a quotation box declares that union president John L. Lewis was the "Babe Ruth of the labor movement." Wilbur MacLean's short comment on his father encapsulates a life (see Fig. 12.16, p. 167). A young man's willingness to brave icy waters results in an old man's pain. Sometimes a person can be brought to life through his or her own quotable words. When researchers find no useful quotations for a topic, they can always quote themselves, pulling an interesting sentence or two from the text they have written and presenting it in larger type. Magazines do this routinely to draw a reader's attention to an article or story.

Fig. 12.16. Quotation Box

> When gold was discovered in California, my father became a Forty Niner. Dad washed his gold out of icy mountain streams. His rheumatism from this made his last days very painful.
>
> —Wilbur MacLean, Joseph's son, in a letter to Wilbur's grandson, Harold.

Visuals for Oral Reports

Oral reports are verbal affairs. Visuals add another dimension, allowing students an additional way to present and process information.

Interactive Displays

Any of the visual formats outlined above can enhance an oral report. Because the designer has the opportunity to actually present the display, he or she also has the opportunity to increase the impact of a visual. Too often a poster is propped up or graphic shown on an overhead and then ignored during a student's presentation. Visuals should be an integral part of the presentation, not some superfluous add-on to fulfill a requirement. Assessment criteria should make this clear (see Fig. 14.3, p. 187).

One of the best ways to make a visual part of a presentation is to interact with it. Students can draw the lines or color in the bars on a graph. They can write on a map. They can add pieces to a pictorial representation one by one. Before uncovering the columns in a table, they can involve the audience by asking them what they expect to see.

Memorable Images

Students wore costumes to give their biographical reports, but the class knew something special was about to happen when Daphne marched to the front of the room tied to a cardboard stake and surrounded by a ring of paper flames. "I am Joan of Arc," she announced. Question Daphne's audience today, and most will still remember that Joan of Arc was burned at the stake. Many are likely to remember why. Daphne had found an inspired image that made Joan of Arc exciting to her classmates.

Several other students had added clever touches to their costumes; Einstein, for instance, wore an unkempt, white wig. Only Daphne and an Elizabeth Cady Stanton, who toted a sign proclaiming, "Votes for Women," had presented images that advanced the story they wanted to tell and emphasized the points they wished to make. Such inspiration will probably not visit all or even most students, but they should be given examples of memorable images and allowed to choose this option for a visual aid. Assessment criteria must emphasize that such dramatic touches must support and advance the information, not merely entertain and amuse.

Not that they can't be entertaining and amusing as well. In a health class, a "doctor" in a suit explained hemophilia to a mustached "Geraldo." He had made his entrance lugging two plastic milk jugs filled with red fluid. He placed one jug in a basin and punctured it; the red fluid squirted into the basin until the doctor stopped it with something he called a clotting factor (really putty). This, he told Geraldo, was what happened during normal bleeding; the clotting factor soon stopped the flow of blood. Hemophiliacs, he added, did not have this clotting factor. He then placed the other milk jug in the basin and punctured it. As the red fluid continued to flow, he explained that this was what happened when hemophiliacs bled.

Realia

Realia often means something from a relative's attic or a treasured collection. But with some imagination, students can invent their own realia. To show how a poor student might have dressed during the Depression, Yolanda wore a burlap shift she had made from a flour sack. As she spoke, she pulled out the newspaper with which she had lined her dress. "It's great insulation," she declared. "It keeps me warm." She then proceeded to take off one of her shoes. They were an old pair and she had punched holes in the soles. She removed the cardboard with which she had lined them, and peered at her classmates through one of the holes. They stared back, wide-eyed and riveted.

To demonstrate the artistic challenges faced by Audubon, Jamaal pointed to a very large stuffed bird that he had borrowed from a science kit. Then he unrolled a sheet of paper. It was large, but not large enough to hold a full-sized drawing of this bird in its erect posture. This was the size paper Audubon used, because it was the size used in the books that would contain his prints. Jamaal explained that Audubon never made birds bigger or smaller, but drew them exactly the size one would find them in real life. He then presented a number of Audubon prints with birds in unusual positions—a swan appeared to be trying to reach its foot with its bill, a crane bent its long neck backwards toward its tail feathers. "See how clever Audubon had to be to fit these birds on the paper," Jamaal exclaimed.

Not every student will be as clever as Jamaal or Yolanda, but if given examples of the possibilities, some will rise to the occasion. Again, it must be emphasized that realia should always help a student communicate important information.

A FEW GENERAL DESIGN PRINCIPLES

In designing visual displays, follow the KISS principle: Keep It Simple, Sweetheart. Use the fewest colors necessary. Consider whether muted tones will communicate a message more precisely than brilliant and possibly distracting ones. Avoid the complicated, decorative fonts that computers offer in abundance. Computers, with their odd type faces and bright colors, can be the enemy of the KISS principle. Visual displays should be pleasing to the eye, but their primary purpose is to communicate.

The first thing a designer must do is identify the purpose for a graphic. Every element of the visual ought to support this purpose. Bright colors should emphasize the most important points; so should thick, bold lines—do not waste them on borders or grids. Sometimes there is a temptation to include everything the researcher knows whether it is relevant or not. A visual should contain only the data necessary to make a point.

Middle school is an ideal time to introduce students to the techniques for displaying information visually. Students should develop an understanding of how visuals facilitate the presentation of information, practice extracting information from visuals, and try their hands at presenting information through visuals. To do this, they will need an awareness of the particular virtues and uses of the different formats.

In terms of design principles, it is enough, at this level, that students recognize that all graphics must have an informational purpose, and that the simplest design usually presents information most effectively. Entire books have been written to identify and elaborate on more sophisticated principles underlying the visual display of information. For anyone wanting to know more, the references at the end of this chapter make a good starting point.

TEACHING THE VISUAL DISPLAY OF INFORMATION

I began teaching visual communication to improve the design of projects for our school's historical museum. Everything I knew fit nicely into a single class period. As the years passed, I continued to collect and analyze examples of visual formats. I began to see that many of the formats merited more in-depth study; this would only be possible if I could locate opportunities for teaming with teachers in a variety of disciplines. My initial teaching experience helped me identify some instructional techniques that I still use no matter what the format or the context.

Instructional Techniques

Show Plenty of Examples

I use a copy stand to turn the visuals in my clipping file into slides. I like to have bad examples as well as good ones so that students will be aware of the pitfalls as well as the possibilities: A map is so colorful that it is almost impossible to figure out what its message or purpose might be.

Tables with too many categories of data make it difficult to know where to begin. Some graphs leave out data any thoughtful viewer would need to draw a conclusion. An initially attractive pictorial representation confuses with an overload of textual explanations in a numbered key.

As students view the slides, I question them. What can you learn about the topic from this graphic? Is there anything you wish the designer had included or left out? If you had to write a title for this visual, what would you call it? What message is communicated with this display? Does this graphic leave you with any questions? What is the first thing you notice? I want my viewers actively engaged in making their own sense of this material.

Examples from my clipping collection are also mounted on posters and some are laminated for individual study. Someday I would like to develop a computer database of visual examples that students can use on their own.

The more my students apply visual techniques, the more they provide me with examples to use when teaching. I now have a collection of outstanding student graphics from past museum displays, as well as some samples of what not to do. Attached to each display is a goldenrod sheet pointing out its particular virtues. I usually arrange the displays around the room and give students time to move around and look at them. Because classes research different decades, I am able to make sure that students do not see any displays related to the decade or topics that their class is studying.

Provide Instruction in the Midst of Research

As I introduce each visual format during my slide presentation, I ask students to identify possibilities for using that format to present information on their topics. As one student puts forward an idea, others begin to see how they, too, might use a particular format. Not every format will work for every topic, but by the end of the class many students have possibilities they want to pursue. Often this leads them to some new research. Now they will need to locate exact numbers or dates or places.

I like to make my presentation about midway through the students' research, because they will have a context for applying what I am teaching. If we examine the visual display of information at the beginning of their research, they have no specific knowledge to relate to the formats. If we do this at the end of their research, it may be too late to find the information necessary to develop a particular type of visual display. Learning about visual formats in the midst of research often provides additional motivation and injects new excitement just when fatigue may be setting in.

Reinforce Effective Use of Visual Displays Through Assessment Criteria

We did not start to see consistently effective visual displays until we took the time to design assessment criteria describing exactly what we wanted. Now, whenever we design a grading sheet for a visual project, we present it at the beginning of the project to identify standards for excellence.

Handing out the assessment criteria again near the end of a project reminds students of all the required elements. Many use it to check that they have met them all. As we all get better at this, I expect our standards to become clearer and more precise.

Teaming Opportunities

I began to realize that students needed a deeper understanding of visual formats than I could give them in just one period. I looked for opportunities to provide more comprehensive instruction.

Geography and Math—The Most Obvious Places

Some of the formats, particularly maps and graphs, were already part of the curriculum. I just needed to convince teachers that discussing the visual display of information would prove a valuable addition to their instruction. Students, particularly middle school students, doubt that what they are learning in school will ever be useful in "real life." Here is proof positive that they can use map and graph skills to communicate more clearly and to understand and evaluate the communications of others.

Teaming offers me additional credibility because I am building on skills students are already studying. Students already know what a key is when I present data maps, and they are likely to be interested in this particular use. We can have an intelligent discussion of scale. They can consider whether a political or physical map will make the best background for a presentation of geographic or historical information. Similarly, in math, we can compare the way the same data looks when presented on both a line and a bar graph.

In a marvelously symbiotic way, I profit from my collaborating teachers' expertise, and they profit from mine. I learn more about graphing, and math teachers learn about its application as a vehicle for communicating information. I do expect there may come a day when many geography and math teachers, having observed my contribution to their units, will ask for my slides and laminated examples and take over the instruction themselves.

The Art Teacher and the Artistic Teacher

The most artistically gifted students produce the projects my eyes are drawn to as I walk the corridors of my school. Here is a striking drawing of a brown bear. There is a diagram that actually makes me want to consider the digestive system. I am excited by the idea that I can show students some techniques for extending their talent to communicate additional information through their pictures. Then they will be able to show me more than just how to recognize a brown bear. I will walk away from the poster of the digestive system with some knowledge of the functions of the different parts and how these parts interact.

An expanded art curriculum now offers me the chance to organize a unit on pictorial representations of information. I will offer many examples of pictorial representations, then have students work from textual information to design their own. Students who find themselves working on research projects in other classes will have the opportunity to consider how they might enhance their projects with pictorial representations.

In addition to artistic students, most schools have one or two artistic teachers. These teachers usually do an excellent job of teaching students how to design attractive research products. Such teachers have a natural interest in visual techniques, and the information formats outlined in this chapter offer them a chance to increase the effectiveness of their students' projects.

Language Arts

The language arts classroom offers students a context for practicing the visual display techniques that use text: the summary box, the highlights box, and the quotation box. Students can begin by practicing on the writing of others, then try to develop summary, highlights, and quotation boxes for their own work. They can compare the results they get from developing summary and highlights boxes both before and after writing. Language arts teachers will be interested in such an exercise if it can be linked to a specific project where it will prove useful.

Science

By the time my students work on their science fair projects at the end of seventh grade, I expect them to have studied and applied at least some of the visual formats in other classes. Science fair offers me a chance to introduce tables, a method for displaying data that many will find useful, and to review a variety of other techniques. When I teach a technique in a specific context, I know I must be alert for later opportunities to teach for transfer.

PREPARING STUDENTS FOR OUR VISUAL WORLD

We live in a society in which information is communicated visually through television, movies, and computers. Such text media as newspapers, magazines, and nonfiction books have become increasingly visual. Just as students need to know how to read for information, so they must also learn to decipher information in visual formats. Just as they need to learn how to communicate effectively through words, so they must also learn to present information in visual formats. Students who learn to present information visually are better able to organize their information, make sense of it, and communicate to others.

REFERENCES

Booth, Wayne C., Gregory G. Colomb, and Joseph M. Williams. 1995. *The craft of research.* Chicago: University of Chicago Press.

Grossman, John, ed. 1993. *The Chicago manual of style*, 14th ed. Chicago: University of Chicago Press. 405.

Tufte, Edward R. 1990. *Envisioning information.* Cheshire, CT: Graphics Press. 31.

Tufte, Edward R. 1997. *Visual explanations*. Cheshire, CT: Graphics Press.

ADDITIONAL READING

Tufte, Edward R. 1983. *The visual display of quantitative information.* Cheshire, CT: Graphics Press.

CHAPTER 13

Creating a Quality Product

An End to Mediocrity

The class sat slumped over their desks; they had been listening to stupefying oral reports for almost half an hour. Now Greta stood before them in a fabulous costume. They expected no less from her. She was a straight A student who always strove to do her best. Everyone waited expectantly for her to begin, but no words came from Greta's mouth. Her face, beneath the broad brim of her feathered hat, was bright red; her eyes were full of tears. Jimmy, the class clown, but also its most sympathetic soul, volunteered to give his report so that Greta might get a drink of water.

Greta thankfully retreated, and declared herself ready to begin when she returned. Her notes shook in her trembling hands, but this time she managed to speak. The students in the back of the room tried to send her encouraging looks, although they could not hear her softly mumbled words. Later, when Greta woefully declared that she had been terrible, her friends insisted that everyone had been terrible. Who had ever heard a good oral report? Well, maybe once in a while one of the stars of the drama club did a decent job, but generally oral reports were a special form of torture.

The teacher-librarian was shocked when Greta reported her disaster. Greta had been so enthusiastic about her research. She had learned a lot, and she certainly had interesting ideas to share.

"You practiced?" the teacher-librarian asked.

"I read my notes at least five times," Greta answered.

"Out loud?" prompted the teacher-librarian.

No, Greta had to admit, she had never actually said the words out loud. Now, thinking about the storytelling unit from last fall, she realized that she should have practiced her speech out loud. With a little effort she would have been able to learn her speech without memorizing it. She should have thought about making eye contact, and varying her pacing and tone of voice. Why, she wondered, hadn't Mr. Steiner reminded them of all the things they had learned in storytelling? Why hadn't he given them any time to practice? One of the most important things Greta had realized from storytelling was the difference practice could make. She was shy and did not have the natural talent of some of her classmates, but she had certainly improved with practice.

The teacher-librarian sighed. She had urged Mr. Steiner to provide some time for rehearsal, but he had been eager to get back to his "regular" curriculum. He was giving up six days for library research, plus the class periods spent listening to oral reports. This was all the time he felt he could spare. Surely preparation of the oral reports could be done as homework.

WHAT DO WE MEAN BY QUALITY?

Too often, students begin their research with enthusiasm and carry it out with interest, only to end by producing dull, uninspired writing or poorly designed, disorganized posters or the sort of deadly oral reports heard in Mr. Steiner's class. Too often, teachers are ready to accept mediocrity in final products as a kind of inevitable doom. Teacher-librarians, having committed so much effort to the earlier steps in the research process, must not fade at the finish line. We must create conditions that support quality final products.

A quality product is one in which a student can take pride. That student knows she has not just met her teacher's requirements, but has also produced her best possible work. She will have improved over her last performance and learned some things to apply to her next task.

A quality product has two ingredients. The presentation should be polished, but a pretty package with no substance does not equal quality. On the other hand, it is simply a shame when students are not given the skills and time necessary to do an excellent job of communicating information that they understand and care about. An audience should be both enriched and entertained by reading, or viewing, or listening to any presentation of student research.

HOW DO WE PROMOTE QUALITY?

Every step in the research process, done well, contributes to excellence. Students must develop research questions they care about, ones that have real meaning for them. Then they will not just be jumping through hoops to satisfy a teacher. Even when students no longer feel they are jumping through hoops, they will still have bars to clear, the bars of high standards embodied in clearly defined assessment criteria. As they pursue their questions and strive to meet the standards, they will need an effective plan that enables them to manage their time well; excellence rarely comes from rushing. A well-thought-out search should lead to resources likely to answer their questions, and perhaps send them digging even deeper. As they reflect on their reading and take summarized notes, they are laying the groundwork for original communication.

Teacher-librarians, having worked so hard to develop the skills for each step in the research process, have two additional contributions to make in promoting quality final products: We can help teachers design assignments that lead to quality work. We can encourage teachers to provide time and coaching for the creation stage at the end of research.

Design Assignments for Excellence

The kind of product that we ask for has a lot to do with what we get. Instead of creating original work, students often copy from an encyclopedia because their teacher has assigned a report. In the students' experience, a report is supposed to sound like an encyclopedia. When I first realized that even capable notetakers might choose to copy from an encyclopedia when faced with the task of producing a report, I realized it was time to ask for something new in the way of a final product.

Change the Product Format

My first stab at alternative formats came when I persuaded a health teacher to offer students some new options for communicating research about a disease. She was not willing to abandon reports altogether, because she feared some students would not be able to cope with the new formats. She was probably right, because we had no plans to teach students anything at all about creating a short story, a child's picture book, a newspaper article, or an illustrated pamphlet. Even so, given a choice, only a fifth of the class opted to do a report, perhaps indicating that many students preferred the opportunity for more creativity.

This assignment evolved through several years and health teachers. Over time, we eliminated reports, pamphlets, and newspaper articles, because they rarely evoked quality work. We now provide writing instruction on developing a story that has an interesting plot and characters, but also includes research. We present models of excellent work done by both students and professionals. We define an excellent final product through clear assessment criteria (see Chapter 14).

A colleague has developed a wonderful metaphor to explain why copied material does not equal quality. She asks students to imagine they have invited someone to dinner. They must find a recipe, then go shopping for groceries, and, finally, cook a delicious meal. In research, the information gathering phase equals the grocery shopping, but just as one would not place bags of groceries in the middle of the table and call them dinner, so one must do some "cooking" to transform the information into an original product. The non-report formats, along with their assessment criteria, provide a recipe for doing that.

Sometimes it does not take much persuading to convince a teacher to change product formats. Take the teacher who told me she never wanted to see another travel brochure in her life. The brochures, she complained, were rarely more than encyclopedia articles in fancy packaging. With only a little prompting on my part, she designed an assignment that would require students to describe a bicycle trip through "their" country. They would describe the terrain of the area they were pedaling through, as well as plants and animals. They would also record the economic activity they observed and describe the people they met. Freed from restrictions of a relentlessly positive travel brochure, they would be able to report on some problems faced by the country.

This teacher was a natural risk taker, and a good thing, too. The first attempt at a new kind of assignment is never entirely successful, but the first attempt yields all sorts of data for revision. What assessment criteria did we fail to identify? What needed skills did we fail to teach? Did students lack prerequisite knowledge or concepts that might have helped them succeed? Which students were most successful, and can we tell why? Risk takers who are willing to suffer through this process can develop first-rate assignments that serve as models for other teachers.

Outstanding ideas for alternative product formats are actually few and far between. Those listed in Figure 13.1 can all provide frameworks for distinctive communication of research findings, as long as assessment criteria are clearly defined and needed skills taught. Whenever you hear of a particularly intriguing new format, be sure to ask about the context in which it was assigned. Often, a good deal of prior teaching will have been necessary for a format to make sense to students as well as appeal to them.

Fig. 13.1. Product Formats Likely to Evoke Original Communication

- Short story
- Children's picture book
- Poem
- Debate
- Magazine feature article
- Advertisement
- Dramatization
- Resumé and job application for a biographical subject
- Museum exhibit

Let me offer one example. A language arts teacher had outstanding success when she asked students to use their research to write a poem. However, she did not simply present a research assignment and tell students their end product would be a poem. First, the class studied poetry, then poetry about "outsiders." Through writing exercises, they identified groups of outsiders in contemporary society and chose one to research. Finally, they each wrote a poem using the knowledge gained from their research. The poems displayed both unusual depth of feeling and depth of understanding. If a poem as final product was simply pasted into another assignment without the preliminary work, the results would not be as good.

Include Tasks That Require Thinking

Good assignment design should focus on major learning objectives. A teacher will also want students to come away from their research with some specific perceptions about a subject. Topics central to that subject should be chosen, ones that will truly deepen students' understanding. The next step involves choosing a product format other than the standard report, to prevent copying. If we also want original thinking, then this, too, must be built into an assignment. We must decide how thinking skills can be incorporated to further learning objectives.

In the Bellevue, WA, public schools, many of us use a model called PIE, Processing Information Environments, developed by fellow librarian, Sandy Koehn (See Chapter 11). For a PIE unit, we create a learning "environment" that provides reasons why information is needed. Key to this approach are tasks requiring critical thinking.

In my school, we have an eighth-grade unit on Native Americans. Before PIE, this was fairly standard stuff. We assigned tribes from different regions to groups, and then asked questions such as: What did they eat? wear? use for shelter? The assignment was not a complete loss, but it never generated the enthusiasm we thought the subject merited—until we placed it in the context of an "environment."

This PIE's central conceit is that a time traveler from contemporary America will visit the tribe in a period before European settlement. Students still learn about food and housing, but now they have to decide what to serve at a welcoming meal, where the traveler will stay, what furnishings he will need, perhaps even with whom he will stay.

A major task involves getting the traveler to the tribe. Since the time travel software is a beta version, the traveler lands at some distance—no more than one state away—and must make his way from there to the tribe. The students have to identify what they need to know to get the traveler to the tribe. Where does the tribe live? (They are not told this.) How do they travel? What would be the most sensible route?

In the old assignment, students had shown where the tribe was located by simply drawing a map on which the main features were the boundaries of modern states. Now, however, students become acutely aware of the terrain. How high are the mountains? Does it make more sense to travel around them? Is there wildlife or weather to warn the traveler about?

Students engage in real problem solving and their solutions are often unique. A Kwakiutl group, convinced they could never give instructions detailed enough to keep the time traveler from getting lost among the islands and bays of Puget Sound, researched all the friendly tribes in the area and had each one convey the traveler for one leg of the journey. A Navajo group imbued their instructions with the tribal values of harmony and acceptance; there were religious ceremonies at key points in the journey. An Inuit group left constructions of sticks and stones to mark their traveler's way.

When I plan a PIE unit, I know I am on the right track if I ask students to *choose, classify, compare, predict.* I need to take a fresh look when I have asked for a lot of simple *finding, listing, recording.* Not every teacher will want to collaborate on a PIE, but many will be willing to integrate thinking skills into assignments by using the suggestions given in Chapter 11.

Think Small

Not every research project has to be a major undertaking. One beautifully simple way to provoke original communication is through brevity. If we tell students they have two minutes to share something genuinely exciting from their research, they will be forced to analyze, evaluate, and synthesize. This must be done with rigor. Use a timer; stop them in mid-sentence. Do it for more than one assignment so they really learn how to do this. The assignment does not have to be oral. Have them write a paragraph, or five paragraphs. It is when we ask for those five-page reports in plastic covers that we get into trouble.

We can also reverse the usual allocation of time for a research project by making the research brief, and spending the bulk of class time on polishing presentation skills.

Provide Adequate Time and Coaching

Creativity and originality are key components of quality. These things may come naturally to a few gifted students, but most students, even those in gifted classes, need time and coaching to create an excellent final product. When teachers plan for research, they often do not block out class time for work on products. When teacher-librarians are co-planners, we must first ask teachers how much time they are willing to devote to a research assignment, and then help them lay out a calendar that includes the production step.

When teams of teachers work together, they can often share the task of promoting quality final products. For example, information gathering might be done with the science teacher; the language arts teacher coaches the writing process; and the math teacher helps with methods for displaying numerical data.

We must be sure students have the skills necessary to produce the kind of final product we are asking for. If they are making a poster, they should first understand the elements of effective poster design, and then practice applying graphic techniques. Specialists, such as art teachers, are often willing to swap classes for a period or two to help a class with presentation skills. When students are to communicate their research orally, the drama teacher or a teacher-librarian with storytelling skills can make a valuable contribution.

As the story at the beginning of this chapter illustrates, rehearsal time for oral projects is absolutely necessary, and yet frequently overlooked. Sometimes classroom teachers feel they cannot provide enough space for the noisy process of rehearsal. Teacher-librarians can help by offering their space when possible. Cafeterias, which sit empty a good part of the day, can also be commandeered.

Many students also require time and space to work on production at school when they do not have optimal work conditions in their homes. In addition to class time, they may also need space and support for working after school (see Chapter 6).

COOKING UP QUALITY

There is a maxim that advises expecting the best from people; this encourages them to become better. It then cautions against being too disappointed when they, in this case our students, do not meet our expectations; this helps them keep trying. Although we must never reward shoddy work, we should target those who do poorly for extra help and support when the next research assignment rolls around.

We must insist that we are looking for quality final products, and that we know all students can produce them. As reflective practitioners, we must also continue to refine assignments until we are satisfied that we have the best recipe for student success.

CHAPTER 14

Assessing Process and Product

The Research Assignment Starts Here

Ben had just received a poor grade on his ethnic heritage project, but he did not understand why. School rarely made sense to him. He could never figure out what his teachers wanted; he just knew that he seldom managed to deliver it. Tamesha's grade was even worse than Ben's, but she was less resigned. She had worked really hard on this project, and now Mrs. Johnson said that almost everything about it was wrong. Mrs. Johnson said she was disappointed; clearly Tamesha had not listened to the directions.

Apparently most of the class had not listened, for almost everyone had received a poor grade. Mrs. Johnson insisted that she had repeated the assignment requirements over and over. When Tamesha protested that Mrs. Johnson should have written down the requirements, the teacher repeated that Tamesha should have listened more carefully. Later, Mrs. Johnson tried to write down her requirements. She found that it wasn't easy. She began to worry; maybe her directions were not as clear as she had thought.

At lunch, Mrs. Johnson's students were astonished to learn that Mr. Ryan had given all his students A's on their ethnic heritage projects. The entire eighth grade had worked on these projects for a Heritage Fair, so everyone had seen everyone else's projects, and frankly the ones from Mr. Ryan's classes did not look that great.

Ms. Suarez's students agreed, but they were beyond astonishment. They were furious. They knew their displays were the best in the fair, but they had not all received A's. When they complained to Ms. Suarez, she explained that she had compared their work to her standards, and not to the work done by other students. The complaints continued. Why did Ms. Suarez's standards have to be so much tougher?

Ms. Suarez angrily declared, "You are in school to learn and improve your skills. What happens with Mr. Ryan's students has nothing to do with that." Then she broke into a broad grin and added, "I am really proud of the work you did, and you should be too."

DEVELOP ASSESSMENTS THAT PROMOTE LEARNING AND GROWTH

If the story ended here, Ms. Suarez would be the heroine, Mr. Ryan a benign villain, and Mrs. Johnson, with her increasing awareness, would fall somewhere in between. But these three teachers, although they had very different teaching styles, liked and respected each other. The Heritage Fair was a new project. They all knew there would be things they would want to change after they had been through the experience once, so they agreed to meet after the project was finished.

I had worked with all three teachers' classes as they did their research for the ethnic fair. When I visited the fair, I made my own assessments of students' work. I looked for common problems, and also noted things that most students seemed to be doing well. When I found an outstanding display that might serve as a model for others, I asked the student to consider giving it to me after the fair. Some students, justifiably proud of their work, wanted to keep their projects, but a reasonable number were pleased to donate theirs. I wanted to raise the issue of assessment at the debriefing meeting, and I knew I could use these examples of excellence as a starting point. They would help me focus attention on the central issue—how could we help all students achieve at a higher level?

Essential Questions

Helping students achieve at a higher level is the primary goal of most teachers. This book is full of suggestions aimed at achieving that goal, but none is more crucial than the idea that we must begin planning for any research assignment by asking some essential questions about how we will assess that assignment.

What Are Our Criteria for a Job Well Done?

In an ideal world, a teacher, or group of teachers, would always sit down with the teacher-librarian well in advance of any research assignment to consider how they might assess both the research process and the final products. Since most assignments begin with a vision of a final product, it makes sense to start here. The assignment might call for a poster explaining a constitutional amendment, or a television news story covering an environmental issue, or a three-paragraph essay examining the work of an artist. Whatever the final product, we need to ask what a well-designed poster or television newscast or essay will look like.

Presentation Criteria. The first answers will probably focus on presentation criteria, and we do not need to reinvent the wheel to identify them. Many districts have writing curriculums that define the competencies a good writer must possess, and these curriculums often contain assessment criteria. An increasing number of states have also established writing standards. It makes sense to use the already defined competencies or standards for all student writing.

Established grading criteria for writing should be used not just for research in language arts but in any discipline, be it science or art or social studies or health. The criteria should be used for the writing component of any project, whether a poster or a television script or an oral report. Not all criteria will apply to every project, and it may even be wise to highlight different criteria with different projects. The writing competency criteria in Figure 14.1 were developed for a history project and are based on the assessment standards of the Bellevue, WA, public schools.

Fig. 14.1. Writing Competency Criteria

- Uses complete and varied sentences. Uses a variety of sentence forms.

- Uses acceptable grammar, capitalization, and punctuation.

- Uses spell checker, eliminates misspelled words, and edits work carefully.

- Writes in a conversational manner and does not sound like an encyclopedia.

- Contains only original writing—*absolutely no* photocopies from books, or printouts from Internet or CD-ROM sources.

Sometimes, you will need to identify additional writing criteria to reinforce a specific type of writing. The last item in Figure 14.1 is one example. When research information was to be presented in a picture book format, a teacher added the criterion, "Must be readable by someone reading at no higher than fifth grade level; no words you need a dictionary to understand." Another teacher, tired of dry, lifeless writing, included the standard, "Would be interesting to someone with no prior knowledge of, or interest in the topic."

Although the skills of reporting orally and communicating visually are likely to be identified as curriculum goals, they are rarely delineated with specific evaluation criteria. Once teachers have worked out criteria for these presentation formats, they should be saved to be reused or reworked by others.

A group of four teachers, who collaborated on a project leading to a historical museum, developed the design criteria shown in Figure 14.2, page 186. As with the group involved in the Heritage Fair, they met when the assignment had been completed to design a common assessment that would support and guide student achievement. After using the criteria once, they reconvened to discuss revisions. All felt frustrated by the omission of creativity on their original list; they found they had no way to reward it when grading. They had also noticed that the best displays used subtitles, but these, too, had been overlooked on the first list of assessment criteria. The teachers agreed that they wanted all students to use subtitles next time. Both subtitles and creativity were now added to the original list.

Fig. 14.2. Visual Display/Design Criteria

- Grabs attention with a headline/title that relates to the CENTRAL PURPOSE.

- Organizes material in a clear, sensible order with a sense of beginning and ending.

- Uses subtitles to arrange and structure information.

- Incorporates contrasting, eye-catching colors.

- Shows creativity and originality in design.

- Demonstrates care and effort in the neatness of the display.

Teachers are most likely to use assessment criteria well if they have been involved in their development. On the other hand, if assessment criteria must always be created from scratch, teachers may often feel they do not have the time to do an effective job. It helps to have lots of varied examples of well-developed criteria to show to teachers who are just beginning to plan an assignment.

Keep a copy of every effective grading sheet developed by a faculty member, and also collect any found during reading of professional books and magazines. A teacher can then pick and choose from among the collected examples and find a style that best matches his or her own style. It is far easier to make revisions or additions than to begin with a blank page. The criteria for oral presentations in Figure 14.3 (p. 187), represent a cut-and-paste assemblage taken from several different grading rubrics.

Fig. 14.3. Oral Communication Criteria

- Makes eye contact with audience.

- Speaks loudly and clearly.

- Uses no nervous gestures.

- Demonstrates enthusiasm and interest.

- Varies pacing to add interest.

- Organizes information in a sensible order.

- Makes effective transitions.

- Uses visuals that enhance presentation and clarify information.

- Interacts with visuals and/or invites audience interaction with visuals.

- Does not read and has not memorized the presentation.

Content Criteria. So far, we have focused on criteria related to a presentation format. But teachers must also consider criteria related to the content of a project, the actual research information that is being presented. These criteria will depend on the learning goals of a particular project, and will vary more from assignment to assignment than presentation criteria.

An art teacher asked students to write a three-paragraph essay about an artist's life and work. The assignment sheet clearly described the information to be included in each of the three paragraphs. The first paragraph was to detail advantages and obstacles in the artist's life; the next was to describe the kind of art he or she created; the final paragraph was to explain what the artist was attempting in a single work of art and include the student's own response to that work.

The first time the assignment was given, it was not accompanied by a grading sheet. About half the class paid attention only to the quantity of paragraphs. Their three paragraphs tended to include standard biographical information about parents and siblings and places lived, plus a list of art works with only occasional mention of the content or qualities of any specific piece.

The next group of students received an assessment form at the beginning of the project. Using it as a checklist while they prepared their projects, students realized that each paragraph must contain the kind of information outlined on the assignment sheet. When they considered the points assigned to the content of each paragraph, they could see that failing to write about the required topics would significantly lower their grades.

The teachers who collaborated on the historical museum managed, over the course of several years, to develop precise criteria (see Fig. 14.4) that reinforced the requirement that a display have a clear central purpose. By insisting upon a number of techniques for organizing the information—summary box, highlights box, specialty visual—they helped ensure effective communication of the central purpose. The criteria not only raised the overall quality of student work, it almost completely eliminated displays that were simply random collections of text and visuals.

Penalizing the inclusion of inaccurate information, and information not in the researcher's notes, drove home the message that the project was to be based on thoughtful, original research. The criteria in the information section were more heavily weighted, in terms of points to be earned, than in the sections on writing and design.

Fig. 14.4. Information Criteria

- Contains a Summary Box—brief overview of topic in paragraph form that draws in the reader, and states a CLEAR CENTRAL PURPOSE for the whole display.

- Covers topic thoroughly by using relevant details and examples. All parts of the display develop and support the CENTRAL PURPOSE.

- Includes a Highlights Box—presents major points of display with bullets.

- Uses at least one specialty visual:

    graph
    map
    time line
    diagram
    quotation box
    definition box

- Provides no information that cannot be found in your notes.

- Contains no inaccurate or incorrect information.

A science teacher liked the final two criteria in Figure 14.4 and included them on her assessment form. She was also anxious that her students pursue the three research questions they had been asked to generate at the beginning of their research. She added this criterion: "Your essay answers your research questions *fully and in detail*." She had identified citing quoted sources as a goal, and so also included, "No copying from sources without using quotation marks, *and* identifying the source."

<u>Process Criteria.</u> Of course, this teacher did not want students to reach the moment when they needed to compose their essays and suddenly realize they did not have adequate information to answer their questions. Nor did she want them to be confused about whether a note contained a quotation. A process assessment would make these things less likely (see Fig. 14.5). The initial assessment evaluated questions, and the next, which focused on information gathering, was repeated three times during library research.

Until now, the points assigned to each criterion have not been included, since they make little sense outside a teacher's specific grading system. Showing them here should give some idea of the impact that failing to meet any criteria will have on a student's grade. Most students are acutely aware of this, and use the assessment sheet as a checklist to make sure they are meeting all requirements. A process assessment form is usually attached to the folder or envelope or booklet in which the student keeps research notes.

Fig. 14.5. Research Process Assessment

PROGRESS CHECK #1

<u>FOCUSED QUESTIONS</u>
- Three approved research questions focusing on important aspects of topic (9 pts)
- Questions written on envelopes of notes folder (8 pts)
- Original, approved questions kept in folder (8 pts)

PROGRESS CHECK #2

<u>FOCUSED QUESTIONS:</u>
- No questions changed without teacher approval (2 pts)
- Original, approved questions kept in folder (1 pt)

<u>SOURCE LOG:</u>
- Quantity _____ (2 pts)
- All sources recorded with complete, bibliographic information, and key symbol (2 pts)

<u>NOTE CARDS</u>
- Quantity _____ (5 pts)
- One main idea per card (5 pts)
- Supporting details for main ideas (5 pts)
- Writing summarized—most information in fewest words (5 pts)
- Notes help answer researcher's questions (5 pts)
- Quotes in quotation marks (5 pts)

Sometimes assignments emphasize particular steps in the research process, and this will determine which aspects of the research process to assess. If a department or a grade level chooses to emphasize certain steps, it will routinely want to include them in the research process assessments. Other types of process assessments can be found in chapters on specific process steps: Chapter 4 for questions, Chapter 5 for planning, and Chapter 9 for notetaking.

What Must Students Know and Be Able to Do to Meet the Criteria?

Both product and process criteria go hand in hand with this important question. If students are to meet rigorous standards, we must determine the skills required to meet those standards. We will have to ask whether they already possess these skills. It is unfair to require that they summarize their notes if they have never done so before. It is not enough to insist that they cite all quoted sources if they are not used to doing this. Once we have identified what students should know to successfully complete a research assignment, we must answer the next question.

How Will We Teach Students What They Need to Know?

Standards make students very nervous if they doubt their ability to meet them. We can lower students' anxiety levels by teaching them what they need to know and by assuring them that they have the skills to meet the standards.

A colleague and I, inspired by a report on performance assessment from the South Brunswick, N.J, School System (Spicer and Sherman 1994), decided to plan for a performance assessment. We quickly realized the absurdity of assessing students without providing needed instruction. We wanted students to work independently over several days. If we did not identify and teach all the needed skills, we could expect many students to struggle and do poorly. It was our job to prepare them for success.

This required extensive planning. Not only did we need to decide what to teach, we needed to determine when and how we would teach specific skills. We would have to provide students with opportunities to practice applying the skills. We realized we would need to connect some of these opportunities to assignments of fairly short duration, perhaps one day's research leading to a paragraph or two. The curriculum was crowded; research had to support existing curriculum goals, not displace them.

Usually, such elaborate instructional planning is not necessary, but the basic principles of identifying needed skills, deciding how to teach them, and providing a vehicle for practice remain the same. Remember the science students who were asked to cite all their sources? I knew we where in trouble when a student rose in indignation to protest that nobody had ever demanded quotation marks around copied material, and she didn't understand why she should have to start using them now. A murmur of approval from the class showed that many agreed.

We needed to prove that it was possible to present research information without unattributed copying. Some instruction on notetaking would help, but I also wanted to give students practice in deciding when to quote sources and how to cite them. After the class had used an overhead to practice the skills together, students individually applied them by using the information from a short article to write brief essays. Everybody received the same article, but students were told to see their responses as original writing. They could make choices about what to include based upon the purpose they each chose for their writing.

They were given the assessment criteria before starting to write (see Fig. 14.6). Although only the first three items related directly to the instructional goal, the others gave students a context for choosing quotations and reminded them of basic research assessment criteria. Since all students used the same article, there was no question about which material was or was not copied.

Fig. 14.6. Citing Quoted Sources

- Most writing is original, not copied.

- Quoted material is so well put that it would have less impact if rephrased.

- All copied material has quotation marks around it, with the source identified in parentheses after the quotation.

- A clear central purpose for the writing is stated.

- The writing focuses on this single purpose throughout the essay.

- Enough information is provided to develop the purpose.

- Information is accurate.

In the best of all worlds, we would be able to identify all needed skills before beginning an assignment. In the real world, we may realize that a skill is needed after an assignment has begun. Sometimes skills can be taught through mini-lessons at the start of each research period. On occasion, it may be worthwhile to take a whole period off if the skill is complex and time can be spared. There will also be times when you will have to wait until you repeat a particular assignment. That is why it is so important to ask these next questions.

How Well Did Our Criteria Work?
What Should We Change?

As you review criteria after an assignment, pay particular attention to the ones students had difficulty meeting. Remember the teachers who collaborated on the historical museum? When it came time to evaluate projects, they discovered that many of their students had done poor jobs of writing summary statements for their research. The lesson on summary statements was developed in response to this problem (see Chapter 9).

In some instances, students may not understand a criterion. It is important to be as clear, jargon-free, and specific as possible. This is not as easy as it sounds; it takes practice. Some rubric writers, in an effort to be precise, spell out four or five levels of achievement for each standard. I do not believe this is worth the effort. As students wade through all the prose, they often have trouble figuring out exactly what their goals should be. The problem is compounded if the rubric is several pages long. One reasonable compromise is to define a standard and then use the terms *always*, *usually*, *sometimes*, *never*.

You will also want to offer examples of work that meets or exceeds a standard, as well as work that fails to meet that standard. Present an excellent summary statement and explain *why* it is excellent. Ask students to examine a poor summary statement and then decide why it doesn't work as well.

However, a word of caution. Sometimes teachers believe it is sufficient simply to show old projects to students. Unfortunately, unless the criteria are clearly spelled out, students will often draw the wrong conclusions. Impressive computer graphics or a pretty cover may overshadow the writing in an essay. An elaborate costume may make the strongest impression during a videotape of an oral report. Bright colors rather than the logical organization of information may seem the key element in a poster.

There will be times when students fail to meet a standard, not because they failed to understand it, but because the bar was set too high. It may make sense to modify criteria for classes with low skills. Such classes often benefit from simpler criteria assessed more frequently, sometimes even daily. The daily reinforcement of meeting the criteria makes students feel successful. A student who is succeeding may tell another who is not, "It's easy, you just do these things and you earn ten points every day." Pretty soon the other student will be earning ten points, too.

It takes time to develop a really good rubric that reinforces product and process goals and communicates standards clearly, yet contains only standards we have prepared our students to meet. Nobody develops a perfect rubric on the first try; three to five revisions are often necessary. Even when you have one you like, it is still wise to review it every time you use it. Kids change, and standards that were once reasonable may assume some underlying skills that are no longer present. Teachers and teacher-librarians change too; we may suddenly have fresh insights about an old assignment.

Purposes of Assessment

The principal goals of assessment are the improvement of learning and instruction. Well-designed assessments help both students and teachers improve. When used effectively, the focus of an assessment is on growth. Good assessments should lead to an understanding by students of what they have achieved, not to competitive feelings of triumph or failure. To promote growth and understanding, assessment must be part of both the research process *and* the product.

Clarifying Standards for Students

Many students do not internalize any standards for research; they see completion of a project and some evidence of effort as all that are required. Others, especially sixth graders, will fall back on the requirements of the past. That is why a flag, a bird, and a flower are likely to turn up on any project about a state, whether they serve a useful purpose or not. And that is why writing is so likely to be copied directly from the encyclopedia, if this has always been acceptable in the past.

Students need to know the grading standards for an assignment at the start of an assignment. They should receive the assessment forms for both process and product before they begin their work. These forms then become guides, alerting students to what they must do to be successful.

We can tell students we want them to take notes that contain a main idea with supporting details; we can provide instruction on how to do this; we can provide models of well-constructed notes; but unless their notes are evaluated by these standards, many will continue to copy information without much understanding. When clear standards are spelled out, most students will do their best to meet them, and even request coaching assistance when needed.

Students with a history of failure often give up before they even begin their research. When they lack clear assessment criteria, they do not understand why they fail; failure just seems to be their fate. If, on the other hand, they receive a poor evaluation because they have left out supporting details in their notes, then they know what they need to improve. They begin to realize that if they ask for help in identifying supporting details, they can improve their grades.

It is only fair to tell students what we require of them. How else can they compose an attention-getting introduction for a speech, especially if disorganized reading from notes has been allowed in the past? How else will they realize that the story of a truck driver's journey through a state should include some elements far more useful than a flag, a bird, or a flower? When we explain our guidelines and apply them seriously during grading, process and products are more likely to meet our expectations.

Monitoring Competency During
the Research Process

When we assess student work during the research process, we offer students chances to get better and to get help. If we wait until research is over and assess only the product, a student may confront failure with no chance to improve. Yes, a student may have gathered inadequate or irrelevant sources, or failed to answer research questions, or taken notes without understanding the material, but it is too late to do anything about it now.

Identifying Students Who Need Individual Help. Negative process assessments should be accompanied by an offer of help. Because students may not be used to receiving process assessments, we must make clear that we are not just deciding how well they have done but are also looking for ways to help them do better. Assessment is an essential part of coaching; we need to decide where a student is now, so that we can help him or her move forward. Assessment during the process allows us to offer coaching assistance when it is needed and when student interest is likely to be high.

The timing of process assessments can vary. When a skill is new, or a particular class is having difficulty mastering it, frequent assessments often work best. If the skills are those students have practiced before, a few assessments at key points—the start, and perhaps one or two other days—may be enough. Or a single early assessment may highlight a few struggling students who merit further tracking. Sometimes the timing of a process step itself, such as searching for resources, will determine when an assessment is necessary.

Process assessments need not be extremely complex. Examining one sample note card from each student gives just as good a sense of whether a student is summarizing as does looking at them all. When possible, stagger evaluations so that you do not have to assess several classes on the same day; this way, you will have more energy for the task. If the teacher-librarian and classroom teacher share the task of process evaluations, there will certainly be more energy, but it is important that both have the same understanding of what the standards mean.

Often the most needy students are the most invisible. They have a knack for disappearing from a teacher's radar screen. To track students during the process, use a class roster on a clipboard with notations that identify students who need help and skills that are giving them difficulty. Or use a set of note cards with names and anecdotal notes about assessments and interventions. Or use whatever works for you to ensure that students who need coaching receive it.

Alerting Students to Areas Needing Improvement. Students, too, can learn to use assessments to figure out what they must improve. They can become like the competitive swimmers who measure success or failure by comparing today's race to previous ones. If they place second or third, or even fifth or sixth, these swimmers are still pleased if they beat their best times. The greatest pleasure comes not from beating others—though no one is likely to turn down a medal. The greatest pleasure comes from becoming better and making progress toward a goal.

If students gain an understanding of the areas in which they need to improve, and then see themselves making progress, they will begin to feel successful, even if they know they will never be top of the class. When assessments are used to promote growth, they can take on a positive role in students' lives.

Detecting Widespread Problems That Call for Reteaching. There is nothing worse than the sinking feeling that comes when evaluation after evaluation shows that many students appear to be missing a skill, or at least failing to apply it. Perhaps they have not used the OPAC for six months and have entirely forgotten how to broaden a search. Perhaps you presented what you thought was a most effective lesson on focused research questions, only to find that half the class seems to have paid the most attention to your examples of unfocused ones.

When most students are having difficulties, individual coaching will not be a viable strategy. It is time to stop and consider how you can reteach a skill. Sometimes the assessments will pinpoint the area of difficulty, and you can solve the problem with a mini-lesson. Often, a simple review of a prior lesson will be all that is needed. On the other hand, if it seems probable that students never really understood a skill in the first place, a different instructional approach may be demanded.

Evaluating and Revising Instruction

Although process assessments occasionally lead to additional instruction during an assignment, product assessments should be carefully considered with an eye to what you might do differently in the future. Perhaps you assumed that a skill was already in place—let's say writing an effective introduction—only to discover that it was not. Or students may have needed a skill you had not even considered when planning the assignment, such as comparing and contrasting.

What you do about these gaps in students' knowledge will depend on the specific situation. A classroom teacher, armed with the knowledge that her students cannot write introductions, may want to provide instruction and practice right then. The teacher and teacher-librarian, having realized that students should know how to compare and contrast, may decide to teach this skill as part of the assignment the next time it is given.

Once in a while, you will probably find that a skill was identified, and instruction and opportunities for practice were provided, but students still had difficulties. Look carefully at all the evidence from both process and product assessments to see if you can find clues to the precise difficulty. Then make your best attempt at revising instruction, realizing that you may have to work again with these students, or on this assignment, to fully comprehend the problem.

Evaluating Achievement and Assigning a Grade

So much has been said about growth and change that you might mistakenly assume that one of the oldest functions of assessment, that of assigning of a grade, no longer applies. That would be wrong. Students, for the most part, take grades seriously; they pay attention to them and want to do well. Grading according to clearly defined criteria helps students make sense of their grades; they are not just seemingly arbitrary numbers or letters. Teachers no longer need to write lengthy comments to communicate exactly why student earned a particular grade. When standards are applied consistently and rigorously, students will be able to understand the reasons for their grades and what they must to do to improve in the future.

And so will their parents. Parents often complain that schools do not have high enough standards. A well-designed rubric can be a vehicle for educating parents about our standards for research. You may want to present a variety of research process and product rubrics at a PTA meeting. Parents need to know that, when a child asks for help with a research project, the first question they should ask is, "May I see the assessment criteria?"

PROVIDE OPPORTUNITIES FOR STUDENTS TO ASSESS THEMSELVES

When students themselves measure their work against clear standards, they begin to develop an awareness of what they can do well and what they need to improve. They are also likely to become more conscious of the steps involved in the research process, and the strategies that will lead to a quality final product.

Although students often use a teacher assessment form as a checklist while they carry out their research and develop their products, they gain a slightly different perspective when they use a self-assessment form after their work is completed. Sometimes you may want to focus their attention on a single skill, or at best just a few skills. Using a simple inverted T-chart for each skill requires students to consider their successes and problems in using the skill and to draw some conclusions about how they will apply it in the future (see Fig. 14.7, p. 197).

If you wish students to evaluate the entire process in a more general way, Handout 5.4, page 58, can be used even when students have not developed a daily research plan. Kuhlthau (1994) suggests asking students to draw a time line of their research process to increase awareness both of their use of time and the steps in the process. A time line will be easier to create if students have kept a journal during their research.

Like process evaluations, product self-assessments can be either narrowly or broadly focused. Use the inverted T-chart in Figure 14.7 when students are to evaluate only one or two facets of their products. Figure 14.8, page 197, contains a sampling of response statements for a more general product self-assessment. Use most or all of the statements for a broad product assessment, or select a few for consideration on inverted T-charts. Starting each statement with "I" encourages students to take ownership.

Fig. 14.7. Self-Assessment Chart

Successes	Failures

Things you've learned that you'll want to do differently for your next project.

Fig. 14.8. Response statements for a product self-assessment.

- I located sufficient resources.
- I avoided collecting too much information from a single source.
- I answered all my research questions.
- I clearly stated the purpose of my project.
- I held to the purpose of my project.
- I presented my information in an order that makes sense.
- I avoided repeating information.
- I provided examples to support my conclusions.
- I used my own words in my writing.
- I used a personal voice in my writing.
- I made my project interesting.
- I worked as hard as I could on my project.

Sometimes you may want to develop response statements that closely match a particular project and its instructional goals. Students, when asked, can also come up with evaluation criteria. Just ask them to identify the qualities that would make a specific type of product excellent.

ASSESS STUDENT LEARNING DURING INSTRUCTION

Everyone has probably had this experience. A lesson seems to go well. The students appear genuinely interested, and they answer the questions you put to them with no apparent difficulty. At the end of the class, everyone works diligently on an activity and applies the skill just taught. Looking over the students' work later, you are stunned to find that more than half have done very poorly. How, you ask yourself, could you have been so wrong about the quality of your students' learning during that class? Now you have two choices. Delay or perhaps eliminate other activities to provide additional instruction, or proceed as planned and hope that students will improve later when you coach them in applying the skill.

This sort of thing is going to happen from time to time. You can make it less likely by assessing student learning while you are teaching. Then you will have the chance to adjust your teaching on the spot, when it is clear that students are having difficulty.

Class Card Sets

I learned a great technique for assessing student learning from a first-year teacher. He had learned it from his mother, who was also a teacher. The first time I asked students a question in one of his classes, they told me I should use "the cards." These turned out to be regular playing cards, each one having a student's name written at the top. When I asked a question, a card would be pulled and a name called by a student who had been assigned this job for the week. The student whose name was called would have to answer the question. Everyone's name was on two cards, so it sometimes happened that a student would be called on for consecutive questions. Every so often the deck was reshuffled.

The effect on the students' interest was powerful. Because a student could be called on at almost any moment, they all stayed focused. There were no complaints that a teacher was either picking on or favoring certain students. Waving one's hand enthusiastically, or trying to become invisible had absolutely no effect. The cards were completely random. The student who selected them took care not to look at the name until a card had been pulled.

I had always prided myself on calling on a cross section of students, not just the eager ones so happy to volunteer the correct answers. I was amazed to discover how much better those random cards were at sniffing out students' confusion. Midway through that first class, a student was unable to answer a question. Another name was called, and another, and another, and another—none had an answer. It was time to stop and poll the class: How many of you think you understand this? No more than a fifth did. I backtracked, trying to find where I had lost them. I asked more questions. I provided new examples. We began to move forward again.

We did not "cover" everything I had planned for that lesson, but most students did understand the things I had been able to teach. I have learned that I need to resist the urge to cover a certain amount of material. If I forge ahead when students are confused, they may be exposed to certain skills, but they will have little chance of mastering them.

Of course, the cards, being neutral, are just as likely to shine the spotlight on student comprehension. The most insecure students are the ones least likely to volunteer an answer, and there are times when, to avoid embarrassing them or to keep a class moving along, I avoid calling on them. The cards give me the opportunity to catch them doing something right, something I can praise. And these are the students who most need praise. The cards, in their own quiet way, help underline my expectation that all students can learn and think.

After my first experience with these students, I knew I had found a worthy use for all those boxes of old catalog cards. I make my own sets of names for other teachers' classes. By blacking out old names each year, I should be able to use these cards for a long time.

Wait Time

Sometimes, if cards do not seem appropriate, I will ask a question and tell students to raise their hands when they have an answer. I add that I will not call on anyone until everyone has an answer. I am signaling again that I expect all students to learn and think.

How long will I wait? The first time I use this technique with a class, I am prepared to wait a long time if necessary. Some students may want to test my resolve. After a while, those who have their hands up will start encouraging the others to "just try." Soon hands should start to go up more quickly. Of course, there will be times when no amount of trying will help some students, and rather than let the rest of the class die of boredom, I will have to call on someone.

If most of the hands do not go up, I know I have a problem, and I will need to adjust my teaching. If all hands go up, but many answers turn out to be wrong, I also have a problem. I try to call on people who have raised their hands both early and late in the process. This approach also works well when there is no single right answer, and I am able to sample several different approaches to a question.

HITTING THE TARGET

Assessment is a key element in the design of research assignments; planning should always begin here. Think of well-defined assessment standards as the colorful rings on a big archery target. When teachers and students can see what they are aiming for, they both know where to direct their energy. Teachers perceive the skills and knowledge students need to complete the assignment, and design instruction accordingly. Students know what is required, and work toward that ideal. Teacher-librarians, in their roles as cheerleaders, must encourage their instructional partners to make assessment the first step in the planning process.

For teachers, the issue of assessment is often linked to the question of time. Do we have the time to design a good rubric? Do we have the time to teach or reteach needed skills, or to slow down instruction when students do not seem to be learning? Do we have time to let students assess their own work? When the answers are no, neither final products nor students' research skills are likely to meet our expectations. Whenever a teacher complains that students' work on research projects proved disappointing, teacher-librarians can turn a problem into an opportunity by offering to help that teacher develop clear assessment criteria for the next project.

If we routinely communicate and apply high standards for research throughout the middle school years, students will begin to understand and absorb the standards for quality work. They will have taken some important steps toward becoming independent learners able to establish their own criteria and live by them.

REFERENCES

Kuhlthau, Carol Collier. 1994. *Teaching the library research process.* 2d ed. Metuchen, NJ: Scarecrow Press.

Spicer, Willa, and Joyce Sherman. 1994. Linking assessment to accountability: Sixth grade performance assessment. In *Assessment and the school library media center,* edited by Carol Collier Kuhlthau. Englewood, CO: Libraries Unlimited.

Sentences to Summarize

The whole class works as a group on these first three sentences when I introduce the skill. I have them on a transparency. Students eliminate unnecessary words, and then volunteer their versions of a summarized note.

The potato is a member of the nightshade family.

He was very handsome when he was a boy.

Salt Lake City was the leading city in Utah from the time of its founding.

The rest of the sentences are for individual practice. Students do four with me in the first class, and three a day at the start of the period after that.

Discus throw was a popular event with the ancient Greeks in their Olympics.

Detroit's park system covers about 6,000 acres and includes more than 200 parks.

In 1938, the slave, Frederick Douglass, escaped from his master and went to New Bedford, Massachusetts.

Dandruff is a condition in which dead flakes of skin are shed from the scalp.

John Muir was born in Scotland in 1838.

A kayak is a wooden boat covered with sealskin and originally used for hunting.

The ayayut, played by Eskimos, is a member of the frame drum family and is similar to a tambourine.

In 1950, there were 4.4 million television sets in the United States.

The first Supreme Court session was held in New York City in 1790.

Pecan trees are native to the southern part of the United States.

Bicycling was a popular fad in the late 1800s.

In 1951, there were 15 million television sets in the United States.

The Alamo was the site of a famous battle between the Mexican Army and a group of Texans.

Huron is the second largest Great Lake, 286 miles long and 183 miles wide.

The Hawaiian Islands were called the Sandwich Islands in the nineteenth century.

Polio epidemics were frequent in the United States from the 1890s to the 1950s.

Mexico City was once the Aztec City of Tenochtitlan, built in the middle of a lake called Texcoco.

A Black Rhinoceros is nearsighted and aggressive and weighs as much as a small car.

Native Americans living in North America numbered 33,000 in 1500 BC.

February is Black History Month as well as American Music Month.

In 1946, Booker T. Washington became the first black man portrayed on a U.S. coin, a commemorative half dollar.

Thirty-five years ago, wilderness lands were formally recognized as an important part of the American landscape with the passage of the Wilderness Act of 1964.

Bake pasties on a cookie sheet at 400 degrees for 45 minutes.

The textile mills of the early 1800s were cold, dark, and noisy.

The Black Death of the fourteenth century, a disease that killed a third of the world's population, was carried by rats.

Ping Pong is considered the national sport of China because so many people play it.

Older houses in China are one story high with whitewashed walls and blue tile roofs.

The two major rivers in China are the Yellow River and the Yangtze River.

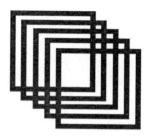

Index

Reading, 91, 117–26
  backtracking during, 120–21, 124
  during presearch, 26–28, 65, 124
  follow-up after, 122–23
  nonfiction versus fiction, 117–18, 124
  promoting nonfiction, 124–26
  and reflection, 18–19, 176
  scanning during, 106, 107, 124
  and signpost statements, 121, 123
  skimming during, 88, 106, 107, 124
  task analysis of, 119, 120–21, 122
  teaching strategies, 123–26
  and thinking skills, 92, 124
Realia, 168
Reference collections, 78–79
Reflection, 8, 141, 181
  and change, 9
  during presearch, 27–28, 65
  mental habits useful for, 19–20
  and reading, 18–19, 176
  subjects for, 10–13
  techniques for, 13–19
Reflective practitioners, characteristics of, 19–20, 181
Rehearsal time, 175–76, 180
Relaxation during presearch, 27, 65
Relevance of information sources, 12, 88, 90, 92, 96, 119, 121–22
Research
  as process, 7–8, 189–90, 193–95, 196
  project formats, 167–68, 177–78, 180
  See also Assessment; Assignment design; Questions, research; Searching for information; Sources of information
Research questions. *See* Questions, research
Rewards, use of, 66, 142
Risk taking, 20, 140, 141, 142, 178

Scanning, 106, 107, 124
Search engines, Web. *See* World Wide Web
Search logs, 17
Searching for information, 7, 45, 59, 62, 69, 71–81
  with CD-ROM resources, 72–74, 75, 76–77, 79, 80–81, 88

  with card catalogs, 72
  with electronic resources, 71–77, 78, 79–81, 87–89
  with the Internet, 72, 74, 75, 77, 80–81, 88
  with OPAC, 71–76, 77, 79, 80, 87, 88, 89
  with print resources, 77–79, 87
  teaching search skills, 74–77, 79–81, 176–77
  using a problem-solving process, 72–74, 77, 81
  See also Sources of information
Sequences, illustrated, 161
Sequencing, 131, 132, 134, 139, 140
Signpost statements, 121, 123
Skimming, 88, 106, 107, 124
Small groups, instruction to, 79
Sources of information
  accuracy, 92, 96, 191
  assessed using thinking skills, 90–96
  assessment, 12, 87–96, 121–22, 123, 131–32
  bias in, 92, 95, 96
  citation of, 188, 189, 190–91
  credibility, 92, 96
  currency, 12, 88, 90, 96, 119
  extracting information from, 121–22, 123
  facts and value claims and opinions in, 92, 93–94, 96, 122
  informational level of, 12, 120, 123
  logic in, 96
  points of view in, 92–93
  readability, 88–89, 90, 96, 119, 123
  reading strategies, 119–23
  relevance, 12, 88, 90, 92, 96, 119, 121–22
  scanning, 106, 107, 124
  skimming, 88, 106, 107, 124
  suitability, 119–20, 123
  understanding, 120, 123
  versus fiction, 117–18, 124, 133
  visual, 120, 121, 145–72
  See also Searching for information
Spaces, work, 67, 180–81
Special education teachers, 68
Special needs students, 68, 79
Storytelling, 175–76, 180